START IT, BUILD IT, GROW IT:
The Contractors Guide to Success

Randy J Brothers

Copyright © 2017 Randy Brothers

All rights reserved. No part of this book may be used or reproduced in any manner whatsoever without prior written consent of the authors, except as provided by the United States of America copyright law.

Published by Best Seller Publishing®, Pasadena, CA
Best Seller Publishing® is a registered trademark
Printed in the United States of America.

ISBN: 978-1-946978-42-4

This publication is designed to provide accurate and authoritative information with regard to the subject matter covered. It is sold with the understanding that the publisher is not engaged in rendering legal, accounting, or other professional advice. If legal advice or other expert assistance is required, the services of a competent professional should be sought. The opinions expressed by the authors in this book are not endorsed by Best Seller Publishing® and are the sole responsibility of the author rendering the opinion.

Most Best Seller Publishing® titles are available at special quantity discounts for bulk purchases for sales promotions, premiums, fundraising, and educational use. Special versions or book excerpts can also be created to fit specific needs.

For more information, please write:
Best Seller Publishing®
1346 Walnut Street, #205
Pasadena, CA 91106
or call 1(626) 765 9750
Toll Free: 1(844) 850-3500
Visit us online at: www.BestSellerPublishing.org

Acknowledgments

This book is the culmination of all the things I have learned in my years as a husband, father, son, brother, business owner, and entrepreneur. It would not be possible if it weren't for the support of the many amazing people I've had the pleasure of knowing along the way.

I want to thank God for giving me the strength and guidance to embrace all the opportunities and challenges that I have encountered along my journey.

Thank You:

- To all of my mentors, coaches and professors. Thank you for guiding me and teaching me the things I needed to start, build, and grow my career.

- To all the amazing people, staff, and colleagues that I get the pleasure of working with on a daily basis. You are the reason for our company's successes and you make it all worthwhile.

- To the amazing family that God blessed me with. I have learned so much from all of you and I am forever grateful for your continued support and encouragement through all of the good times and the bad.

- To my young children: Ryder and Mila, follow your heart, chase your dreams, put others first, do things for the right reasons, and you will find joy and happiness along life's journey. I love you.

- Last but not least, I want to give a special thanks to my beautiful wife, Christina, for her unwavering patience, love, support, and encouragement. You believed in me when I was just starting out and when we had very little. You have stuck with me through thick and thin. You are the reason I wake up everyday with tireless motivation and a relentless desire to succeed. None of this would be possible if it weren't for you. I am blessed to have such an amazing person by my side. I love you with all my heart.

Randy J. Brothers

Contents

Chapter 1   Getting Started 1

Chapter 2   Becoming an Entrepreneur 11

Chapter 3   Understanding the Numbers 19

Chapter 4   It's Not What You Know… 28

Chapter 5   Building the Right Foundation 36

Chapter 6   Hiring the Right Team 46

Chapter 7   Coaching, Training and Leadership 57

Chapter 8   Building a Sales Program 67

Chapter 9   Marketing and Branding 92

Chapter 10 Growing your Company 108

Chapter 11 Transitioning from *In* to *On* 119

CHAPTER 1
Getting Started

There I was, a ten year old kid selling Blow Pops out of my backpack in the back of the school bus. I had figured out that if I used my allowance to buy a box of blow-pops from the grocery store, I could sell them for $.25 cents each and get back more money than it cost to buy them. Within a few days, the bus driver caught wind and shut me down. Despite my first failure in entrepreneurship, I had a taste in my mouth that would never go away.

It wasn't until 10 years later while attending college at the University of Northern Colorado that I learned what real entrepreneurship was all about. I was in my second year of business school and one of my classes featured guest speakers that were experienced entrepreneurs. One speaker told the class a story about how he had built a company that he later sold for $40 million dollars. Hearing that story piqued my interest in entrepreneurship even more.

Another guest speaker talked about how he started a window cleaning company while he was still in college, and it was at that moment that my real entrepreneurial journey began. I knew a life in the business world was meant for me.

The very next day, I called a good friend of mine and we started our very own window cleaning company. Although we had no clue what the heck we were doing, we knew that we needed clients and we knew that our target clients were homeowners. So, we went to the computer lab, created a logo, and printed 100 fliers to put on peoples' doors.

The next day, we went out and put our flyers on as many of the nicest houses in town that we could. We then went down to the local hardware store and bought some ladders, a bucket, some scrubbers and a few other items; we were ready to start up our very own window cleaning company. Shortly after buying supplies, the phone rang and low an behold, we had our first customers.

At the time, we had no clue what to do or even what to charge. We counted all the windows, and decided that we would charge a few bucks per window. The people actually agreed to the terms and off we went. We started early in the morning around 9 o'clock, and since we had no clue what we were doing, it ended up taking us all day. We were finished and out of the house just before dark. By the time we were wrapping up, it was clear that the owners were more than ready to get rid of us having figured out that we were novices. Despite the time it took, and our clear lack of experience, we received a check for $430, and so began life as an entrepreneur.

As a lifelong entrepreneur, I now have a lot more experience than I did back then. I have made many mistakes and learned a lot throughout the years. Through all the lessons learned, through both failures and successes, I have narrowed my experience down to ten rules that every aspiring entrepreneur should know before committing to a life in business.

Ten Rules of Entrepreneurship:

Rule #1: Prepare to be unprepared. You're not going to be ready for everything. It's important to try and anticipate multiple outcomes when making decisions. Plans are going to change. Try and have a plan A, B and C when making plans.

Rule #2: Embrace failure. You're going to fail. It's a hard truth. It's a reality. There will be failures, but failures prepare you for successes. Nearly every successful entrepreneur has failed many times before they found success. Fear of failure can prevent you from getting started, but it can also give you the courage to be great. Embrace it. It's going to happen.

Rule #3: Learn from your mistakes. You are going to make mistakes. Your staff is going to make mistakes. Don't dwell on them and don't punish others for theirs. The best education you are going to get is by learning from your mistakes.

Rule #4: Hire character, teach skills. People are your company's most valuable asset. Understand that and treat them accordingly. People are going to come, people are going to go. As long as you hire good quality people and give them the tools to learn and grow, everyone will succeed.

Rule #5: Opportunity knocks. Opportunity will present itself. You can neither control nor force opportunity. All you can do is work hard and learn new things every day. Stay open minded, learn from every conversation, build as many quality relationships as possible, and opportunities will come.

Rule #6: Change is inevitable. Embrace it. Most people don't like change, and if you don't like change, entrepreneurship may not be for you. A business is a living, breathing entity. It is always growing. It is always changing, and you, the owner, should always be changing and growing with it.

Rule #7: Don't freak out. Bad things happen whether you like it or not. When you freak out, everyone freaks out. Don't focus on the problem, focus on the solution. Make quick, efficient, and logical decisions. Deal with the results as they happen.

Rule #8: Always be learning. Be a student of your business. Be a student of your industry. Understand that you don't know everything. Take advantage of every opportunity to learn and grow every day.

Rule #9: Take the high road. Integrity is everything in business. There will be many times when you'll be challenged, and you will be asked to do things that are outside your ethical comfort zone. If you have to question if something is unethical than it probably is. The key is, always do what you know is right even if it jeopardizes relationships. Unethical people always lose in the end, so why associate with them. Don't burn bridges because you never know what or who will provide opportunity in the future.

Rule #10: Time is your most valuable asset. There are only so many minutes, hours, and days in our lifetime; don't waste time on things that don't propel you forward. Having studied many successful entrepreneurs and read many business books, the one commonality between them all is the level of which they value their time. Time management has been one of the most important keys to my personal success.

Casting Your Vision

Okay, now that we've got my ten rules of entrepreneurship out of the way, let's get started and talk about the business basics. As an entrepreneur, there are innumerable questions to ask yourself and countless things to do to get your business off the ground. I call this *casting your vision*. Whether you like it or not, you have to be a visionary for your company. For some people, this is not natural. Some folks just don't naturally cast a vision, or may not know what this even means. They don't naturally have the ability to be a visionary, but it can be a learned process. This is an example of why it's important to take the necessary time to sit, think, and process exactly what you want to do and what it will take to get it done.

Being passionate and understanding your industry are important keys to casting an achievable vision. Knowing your industry inside and out is essential to casting a vision to your employees. I already spoke about being a student of your industry, but it's also important be a student of your product as well. You'll improve your chance of success if you build a business around something you know inside and out, and that you're passionate about.

Casting a vision starts with establishing a goal that your whole company can work towards. It can be a financial benchmark, an industry achievement, or rating that you want everyone to strive for. For example, "Our goal is to be the #1 rated company in our state and we strive to achieve that goal by providing the best customer experience possible." As Stephen Covey stated it in his book *The Seven Habits of Highly Effective People*, "Begin with the end in mind."

Once you've established a vision, your next concern is to determine how you're going to execute that vision? How are you going to get to that end you have in mind? How are you going to get your business built to be a successful, well-oiled machine? The short answer is to find the right team and get everyone on that team working together towards achieving the vision that you put forward.

Partnerships

In my experience, having a partner is an important key to building a big, successful organization. While individually you may have a vast knowledge of your industry and have many strengths and few weaknesses, one person is only able to handle so many of the responsibilities and requirements that it takes to build a great company. I have had the best success when I've had a strong partner in my businesses.

There are a few things to consider when looking for the right business partner. It's imperative that you thoroughly vet your prospective partner. Make sure they have a good history of ethical and honest business practices. It's a good idea to find a partner whose strengths can balance your weaknesses. The ideal partner should have a different, but complementary personality to yours. A business with two type A personalities is most likely destined for failure.

The most important factor to consider is trust. At the end of the day, many business decisions come down to your gut feeling. A business partnership is like a marriage. You'll want to choose a partner that you trust without reservation—someone with whom you feel you could spend all the time necessary to build a successful business with. Whether you're planning to keep it in the family forever, or you're building a business to sell, you will both need to be on the same page and trust one another 100 percent.

Funding

Now that the vision is cast and the partnership is established, it's time to get your business funded. Inexperienced, uninformed people think that to start a business they first must go raise a large amount of money. Their approach to getting their business started is to throw money at different things with the hopes that something sticks. Their intention is to figure it out as they go. I don't look at it that way. The proof of concept theory is a much safer approach.

Proof of concept happens when you prove that your business model works and that your industry has a demand for what you are selling. Using this approach, you're better off getting your business started with as little expense as possible. In the home improvement industry, you must first make sure you have the ability to execute and deliver a good-quality service and product on time, on budget, and for the right price. It's a good idea to do this before you go spending a bunch of money on hiring, marketing, and branding.

The reality is, once you know that you have a good business model and that there are customers that want the services you provide, it does take money. There is an old saying, "It takes money to make money." It's going to take money to get started and to grow your business. The next question is, "how much money is needed?"

When I first started my roofing company, I did some basic math and figured out that in order for me to get through three month's of work, I would need $25,000 cash and a credit line to purchase materials, or so I thought. Little did I know I was substantially underestimating the amount of money that it would cost to actually get my business up and running.

There are a variety of ways to get funding. Most people first tap their own savings, a mortgage, or other resources before asking their friends and family for money. If that doesn't provide the necessary funds, the next option is to get a loan from a bank. You should plan to bring your business plan to the bank with you. Do be advised that this route is difficult when you are just getting started, you haven't proven your model, or you don't have a history of successful business. Good luck getting any money from a bank.

The next option to get money for your company is through private funding, or what is referred to as hard money. There are many private investors out there. It's important that you take only what you need and that you get the lowest interest rate possible without giving up equity in your company. Construction companies usually start out small, but you will need money to be able to get your projects underway. You'll need funds for marketing, to build a website, for inventory, and many other things. An investor is going to charge anywhere from 10 to 30 percent interest depending on the agreement you make. The interest rate will be determined based on things such as: how soon you're paying it back, how much risk they're taking, and how much money they're investing.

When you take money to fund your company, you need to recognize that you're going to have to make sacrifices. You're going to have to do whatever it takes to make your business happen. This isn't a situation where you can just set up a GoFundMe page to start a roofing, painting, or general contracting business. People don't want to invest in these sorts of businesses because they have such a high failure rate. The moral of the story is, if you plan to start a business, begin with a good analysis to determine exactly what it's going to take to get your company started and keep it going. You want to have at least three to six months of funding in place to be able to procure materials, get the marketing in place, and get the things you need done in order to get your business off the ground. Many times, you'll have to reinvest your earnings back into your company in order to grow.

Many of the most financially successful entrepreneurs started with very little capital and worked their way to financial independence. Daymond John, one of the investors on the popular television series *Shark Tank*, has authored a book *The Power of Broke*, in which he details 15 very successful entrepreneurs who came from very humble beginnings. Daymond John, himself, started out selling t-shirts from the back of his van. He had a vision of a clothing company geared towards young men. He focused on proving that model, reinvesting in his company and he grew it into a multi-billion dollar industry phenomenon.

Licensing

The next consideration to make when getting your new construction business started is licensing. Nearly every city in the country or the world has building codes and regulations. Make sure that you have the proper licensing—not only business licensing, but also contractor licensing. If you're going to specialize in a certain type of construction, you're going to want to make sure that you meet the requirements to obtain the license in the jurisdiction, county, or state you're working in. There are different requirements between the jurisdictions throughout the country so check with your local building department before conducting business.

Before I got my first contractor license, I went to the local community college that offered a course on International Residential Code (IRC).

That class taught me an understanding of building codes and how to navigate my way through a two-inch-thick code book. It also helped me prepare for a four-hour licensing test. I had to meet those requirements to get my very first contractor's license, which allowed me to get my first construction company off the ground. Be careful. You don't want to dive right in and start a construction company if you don't have the proper licensing and registrations in place. Improper licensing can derail your business before you even get started.

The Business Plan

When I first started my construction company, I sat down and I hand wrote out my business plan on a sheet of paper—two pages front and back. It was basically just a list of everything I could think of that I would need to do to launch my business. It was primitive, but that's how I got started. As the saying goes, hindsight is twenty-twenty, and if I knew then what I know now, things would be very different. What I've learned is that if you're going to start a business, a business blueprint is vital.

There are six main components to consider when developing a plan for your new business:

1. Planning and Budgeting: This is the process of setting up a method for tracking and analyzing critical numbers within your model in order to create a budget for your business. You will also want to use these critical numbers to determine what the key performance indicators (KPI) will be within your business and to plan your business growth.

2. Organizational structure: In this section you will want to determine what roles, duties and responsibilities you will need to get your company started and which ones you'll need to help it grow. Try and envision what your company will look like 1, 3, and 5 years from now. Illustrate what that looks like on a bubble chart

to create a tangible organizational structure to help visualize what that company will look like at each phase of growth.

3. Recruiting and Hiring: This section should be focused on creating a standardized process of recruiting, interviewing, hiring, and onboarding your staff as you grow your company.

4. Training and Coaching: In this section you'll want to create a method of training and coaching your staff on an ongoing basis by way of structured meetings and direct reporting.

5. Marketing and Sales: Establish a marketing strategy and budget in this section. Build a plan to execute your strategy with a specific timeline. Create a standardized sales process that starts when the phone rings and ends when the customer is satisfied and paid in full.

6. Goal-Setting and Priority Management: In this section you will want to establish a method of setting, tracking, and measuring goals for yourself and for your entire staff. You will also want to create a schedule that blocks out specific times for you to work on priorities with a focus on improving and growing your business.

Once you've developed a plan that includes all six of these categories, you're ready to start your entrepreneurial journey. It may seem like a daunting task, but you will save yourself many headaches and grow your company much faster with a well written and well executed business plan.

What I learned from my first business venture is that all it takes to get started is an idea, a plan and a lot of knocking on doors. You don't have to know everything about a business before you get started; just have the courage to jump right in. Find something you can be passionate about, cast your vision, be ready for some hard work and you'll be ready to start your entrepreneurial journey.

CHAPTER 2
Becoming an Entrepreneur

I didn't have all the answers when I became an Entrepreneur and still don't. Every person is different and every entrepreneur has different motivations. The one thing we all have in common is that we strive for success. I believe that I was born to be an entrepreneur and I also believe that there is an entrepreneur in all of us. We just have to figure out how to harness our business ideas and put them into action. If you are reading this, chances are you can relate.

Growing up I knew I wanted to be a businessman but I didn't have a clue where to start. All I knew was that I wanted to learn as much about business as possible. I made sure to find a college that offered a business degree and that would accept my marginal grade point average and test scores. I was blessed with the opportunity to attend the University of Northern Colorado. It wasn't easy at first. I wasn't a big fan of school growing up. I didn't do well with authority and my ADHD made it difficult to focus. I just had to figure out how to get good enough grades to get into the business program.

It wasn't until my junior year that I figured out what industry I wanted to be in. As a kid, I always loved trucks, cars, and anything with a motor that went fast. I subscribed to *Motor Trend* and *Hot Rod* magazines before I could even drive. I dreamed of having fast cars and big trucks. I knew lifted trucks were expensive and noticed that many contractors had them. I figured, "if contractors could afford lifted trucks then they must make money, right". The connection might not sound too logical now, but it made sense to me back then.

My Father and Grandfather were skilled carpenters and I was always fascinated with how things were built. I had a knack for building things from early on. They had had a few different construction and roofing companies growing up and I got to learn a lot at an early age. It all made sense, so I decided that I would focus on the construction industry. After watching how hard my father and grandfather worked their whole lives, I knew that I wanted to learn construction in a different way. I wanted to learn the business side of the construction industry. I wanted to get to the top without spending a lifetime with a hammer in my hand.

As luck would have it, a friend of mine from high school and college mentioned that she had just gotten a receptionist's job at a local construction company. I had no other contacts in the construction industry, so I proceeded to bug her for the next six weeks to get me an interview. After weeks of persistence, she finally got me an interview with her boss.

There I was, a 20 year old kid with no experience and no real plan, trying to convince a stranger to teach me how to build a house. In the course of 2 hours I managed to BS my way through the interview. I did my best to sell myself as a person who wanted to learn this industry and was willing to work hard. I even offered to work for free. I pleaded my case as best I could, but I walked out of that meeting empty handed. We had a great conversation and I learned a lot, so it was worth it either way.

The very next day, I got a call back from the owner. He said that he didn't need a project manager since his partner managed all the projects. However, he said he was building his own house, and that he could use an assistant to help him with his personal project. I didn't have a clue if I was going to make any money or what kind of work I would be doing. I just said yes.

Confidence and Self-Awareness

When I walked into that office and got my first construction management job I didn't walk in with experience or knowledge. I walked in there with confidence. Confidence that if I was straightforward with my eagerness to learn and understanding of my lack of knowledge that I could get that job. I was given that opportunity because I was able to overcome my fear of rejection with confidence to achieve the objective I had set forth in my mind. We have to overcome the fear of failure and the fear of rejection before we embark on this entrepreneurial journey. We have to use that fear as fuel to give us the confidence to succeed.

I wish I would have been more self aware when I was starting out. I would have avoided so many mistakes. Self-awareness is very important but not discussed enough. Our industry is made up of a wide variety of personalities with many different backgrounds. Many contractors start their own companies because, after years and years of working in the field, they are tired of working for someone else. They know everything about their craft so why make money for someone else when they can make money on their own. The majority of trades companies are made up of two backgrounds, they either come up as a worker or a salesperson. What we fail to understand is just because we're great at sales and/or great with our hands doesn't mean we're great at business. Trades businesses fail because of lack of self awareness, not lack of knowledge.

In order to get better at understanding your business you need to get a better understanding of yourself, first. You can install a roof, you can build a house, but how do you turn that into a profitable, sustainable business? In order to get yourself to that place, you have to ask yourself some tough questions. Who are you? What really motivates you? Are you a greedy person? Are you a selfish person? Are you naturally empathetic towards others? Are you detail-oriented? Are you a controlling person that has to micro-manage everything? What are you really good at, and what abilities do you lack? Once you can get a true grasp of who you are and what your real strengths and weaknesses are, you can put others in place to focus on the areas that you are lacking.

We're entrepreneurs. We're leaders. We're the head of our companies, therefore, we're expected to have all the answers. That's the pressure that no one talks about. The reality is that just because we're owners, we don't know everything. Nobody knows everything. As long as we are self aware and we recognize that learning is a continual process to achieve growth, we should have everything in place to be able to get our businesses off the ground and off to the next level.

A great book that I would recommend on this topic is *StrengthsFinder 2.0* by Tom Rath. By answering a series of questions, it helps a person to uncover and assess their talents. A person's characteristics are measured against 34 types of talents or strengths to indicate an individual's applied productivity or propensity to succeed in a particular area. If you're not good at something, you're far better off finding somebody to do that task who seemingly is good at it, and you should focus in on being great at the things you are good at. I know it seems a bit backwards from traditional thinking. We naturally want to focus our energy on getting better at the things we are not good at, but what would happen if we delegated those things and shifted our focus to the things that we are already naturally good at?

I am a Type A who naturally wants to be in control of each situation. Leadership is one of my greatest strengths. I also have a high risk tolerance and an idealistic mind that sometimes gets me carried away with chasing business ideas that I shouldn't be chasing. I call it, chasing rabbits. This book helped me narrow my focus and stay in my lane. I know that I am terrible at follow up, organization, paperwork, and details, so I make a point to hire and partner with people who are naturally great at these things.

Find Your Why

What is your why? Why do you do what you do? Why are you in business? Why does your company exist? Why do you work for whom you work for? Is money your main motivation? Do you want freedom? Do you want to take care of your family? Do you want to increase your quality of life? Do you want to work less and make more? Do you want to work more to make more? Do you want to feel like you're getting a value out of your work? Do you want to create jobs? Do you want to inspire others? What deeply motivates you? These are questions only you can answer.

I hadn't really put much thought into my "why" until I read the book *Start with Why: Why Great Leaders Inspire Everyone to Take Action* by Simon Sinek. Although I came across that book randomly, it completely changed my life. Before I read it, all I cared about was what others thought of me, how cool my truck was, how many toys I could have, and how much money I could make. When I started asking myself these hard questions to try and figure out exactly why I do what I do, it became clear to me that money, trucks and toys were not my primary motivation. I don't do what I do for the money. For me, I really want to help teach and inspire others, so in the simplest form, my personal why is to gain success by helping others succeed. I believe that if you help others succeed, and focus your efforts on putting others first, great opportunities will follow. One of the first things I learned in business school was if you want to be a successful entrepreneur, you need to find people who are better than you.

Once you figure out your "why" you want to develop a statement that defines your why. For instance, Apple's why is "to challenge the status quo". Now, take the things that you've learned about yourself and about why you do business, and use them to create your company's core principles. Try to focus on whatever is closest to your heart and motivates you the most. Your "why"needs to be directly incorporated into your company's culture. I'm a firm believer that a company is a direct reflection of its leadership. So, the more we focus on ourselves, and the more we learn and grow and get coached and coach others, the better off we are as contractors, people, and leaders.

Core Values

On my journey to understand myself and understand my why, I was able to narrow down to four core values that I not only live by personally, but that we also have incorporated throughout our entire company. The first of my core values is faith. I was raised in a conservative Christian home. My stepfather was a pastor and my mom was always involved in ministry work. Being raised in a Christian home taught me about faith in God which made it pretty natural to use as my first core value. Faith is more broad than just faith in God though. In a broader sense, you need to have faith in yourself, have faith in your journey, and have faith in the people around you. If you believe that you will be successful, then the people around you will believe it also.

The second principle I adhere to is family. This one is tough because everybody has different family history. We all come from different backgrounds; some positive, some negative. Some people have gone through a lot of hardship when it comes to family, others not so much. Many small companies involve working with family. Regardless of your family background, family is important. Whether you have a lot of family or not, it's a good idea to treat customers as if they are your family.

Honesty is the third principle I live by and infuse in my companies. It really goes without saying. You're never going to be a successful entrepreneur if you're not honest. To be blunt, if you lie, cheat, steal, act deceitfully, or do anything to better yourself over somebody else for the wrong reasons, you're dishonest and you're going to fail. Always be honest in everything that you do. The straight shooter always wins in the end. Honest.

Integrity correlates directly with honesty. As I talked about in the last chapter, and as you embark upon your entrepreneurial journey, what you'll be challenged with most is your integrity. Undoubtedly, many times you will be confronted by situations where the unethical route might seem easier. Believe me, it never works out in the long run. Just take the highroad.

Ethics

Entrepreneurship is about making deals. Deals with clients. Deals with employees. Deals with other entrepreneurs. When doing business deals, every agreement needs to be ethical, honest, and straightforward. A good agreement leaves all parties feeling as if they got a fair outcome. My rule of ethics when making deals is; "if you have to question whether it's ethical, don't do it". It's not worth it. There will always be a better deal to come later on down the road.

You're going to make mistakes and you're going to get the short end of the stick sometimes. You're better off learning from the mistake than recanting on a deal. No one wants to do business with someone that doesn't stand behind their word. If you make a mistake that costs you financially, deal with it. Don't try and place blame on others. When you get into a financial pinch, don't tuck your tail and hide. Deal with it head on. Just take ownership and be straightforward with yourself and the other part involved. When costly mistakes happen, I usually just pay for them. Many times it's not worth the time or the hassle to recoup money on petty things. There's no point in burning bridges in this business because you never know what's going to come back around in the future.

My first real "deal" on my journey to become an entrepreneur was one where I was willing to work for free to gain knowledge. I have made many deals since then. Many have worked out and many have not. Either way, I continue to make deals and I continue to learn and grow while chasing my dreams. To me, that's what being an entrepreneur is all about.

Entrepreneurship does not have a specific definition. I became an entrepreneur when I took the first step towards chasing my dream. Remember why you are starting your company. Remember what your big picture dream is. Learn and grow everyday. Chase your dreams with relentless passion and an unwillingness to quit and you too will become an entrepreneur.

CHAPTER 3

Understanding the Numbers

I had two-and-a-half years of general contracting experience and a business degree when I first started my company. I thought I knew everything and I was determined to make it happen. I dreamed of being a custom home builder, but I knew I couldn't afford to build a house at the time. So, I decided that I would begin by doing remodeling work. My intention was to do some basement finishing work while working my way to building custom homes. I started with basements because I knew that a lot of houses had been built with unfinished basements in the past few years and there were a lot of people in the market for basement finish at the time.

    I had reached out to a few subcontractors that I knew to let them know what I was doing. I asked if anyone knew of any potential customers. It turned out that my drywall guy had been approached to bid a complete finish that same week. He didn't know the management side and he could get the drywall and paint done at cost. We decided to work together on it and figured that we could split the profit at the end.

    Although I had no clue what I was doing, I went in, measured everything, and re-measured it all once more just to make sure. I spent hours putting together that bid. I wanted to get it right. I had some experience with bidding with the previous company, but not enough to be confident bidding jobs for my own company.

At last, I put together the bid and presented it to my clients. They looked it over and proceeded to ask a ton of questions. They asked about finishings, floor coverings, paint colors, fixtures etc… I was so excited that they didn't take the bid and get rid of me that I started answering their questions and saying yes to things I shouldn't have been saying yes too. I walked out of there with a signed contract and a smile on my face. I didn't care, I had gotten my first job!

Here we go, we're off and running! I am the owner of my very own construction company. I had made it. I projected a 6-8 week time line which took nearly 12. I budgeted for approximately $15,000 in costs and had sold the project for $20,000. By the end of the project I had spent over $18,000 and was left with no real profit at the end. I chalked it up to the learning curve and figured I'd make it up on the next one.

Luckily, I started getting more and more basements to finish. I had hooked up with an investor that was buying houses, finishing the basements, and flipping them. I was doing two or three projects at a time. It wasn't until I was already a year in and had finished a handful of projects that I started noticing that nearly every project wasn't as profitable as I thought it would be. I was making hardly any money at all. I was barely making enough money to survive, let alone pay for my bills, my housing, my office, my fuel, my materials, and other expenses. The problem was I didn't know my numbers. I knew construction, and I knew how to manage a project, but I didn't know how to analyze my numbers.

Accounting Basics

Before anything else, it's a great idea to have some type of accounting software. There are several choices, *QuickBooks* is a very popular one. I use *QuickBooks Contractor Edition* and it may be a good idea to start with it or something very similar. Make sure you have a familiarity with the accounting software you choose. There are many training options with each one. You will at least need to know how to track things and write checks when you first start out. You will definitely want to have a bookkeeper and a CPA, as you grow, but it's on you in the beginning. Eventually, you will want to have someone in charge of the finances who is competent and trustworthy.

Disclaimer: I am an entrepreneur not an accountant or a bookkeeper; they are much smarter than I am. I have learned about accounting and finances the hard way. Consult your accountant for the correct recording and reporting methods for your business.

It's important to have, at minimum, a basic understanding of what the main financial metrics are for your business model. You will need to know what reports you should be looking at on a regular basis. You will need to understand these numbers in order to make strategic decisions as you grow your company. Here's my version of accounting basics. It starts with total sales (Revenue) and it ends with net profit... or loss.

Terms

Total sales (revenue), is the total amount of income generated by your company. It is the top line on your company's income statement. For example: If you sold one job in a year for 10k your total revenue would be 10k. If you sold 10 jobs at 10k each your total revenue would be 100k.

Costs of Goods Sold (COGS) are the direct costs directly tied to the goods or projects that have been sold. They are usually made up of the direct labor and material cost on a project. They are important to track on each job and are essential when trying to budget for fixed costs and to project growth.

Gross Profit (GP) is the profit the company has produced on each project before considering the fixed costs. It is calculated by subtracting the COGS from the total revenue. It is also known as gross margin.

Example: (Revenue) =100k - (COGS) 65k = (GP) 35K. Essentially the GP is now your operating budget to conduct business outside of the direct or variable costs tied to each project.

Fixed Costs (FC) are the total of all the remaining costs of doing business—otherwise known as overhead. This is where your salary, your staff's salaries, and other costs such as insurance, fuel, and vehicles are accounted for. Fixed costs stay relatively the same each month. You can change your total fixed costs to help you increase the bottom line or net profit.

Net Profit (NP), otherwise known as *the bottom line*, is calculated by subtracting the total fixed costs from the gross profit. Net profit is the total amount of money your company makes or loses within a given time period. It is also referred to as net margin. Example: (continued) GP = 35k Let's say the total fixed costs (FC) = 25k. (GP - FC = NP= 10k). Your company made a total net profit of 10k. This may seem like an elementary example of basic accounting but these example numbers provide a great basis for many construction company models.

Depending on how your company's business model is set up and what your primary focus in construction is, you can adjust these numbers to set some reasonable starting points for your own business development. If you have a highly labor-intensive business model, such as a trades company or painting company, you may be able to adjust your direct or variable costs down a bit. You are not paying more for subcontractors and you can save on labor. You will have a higher GP, but you might incur higher fixed costs with the increased insurance premiums and added vehicle maintenance costs. If you own a general contracting company or a similar business model that contracts out labor, like many roofing contractors, you might have a lower GP but also have lower overhead because your subcontractors aren't costing as much tax or insurance money. You can also avoid vehicle and fuel costs. Use this as a good starting point and adjust your numbers as you acquire more data. Here's the whole example again including percentages.

Total Revenue / Sales = $100,000 (100%)

Less: (COGS) Total Variable costs= $65,000 (65%)

Gross Profit (GP) = $35,000 (35%)

Less: Fixed Costs / Overhead = $25,000 (25%)

Net Income / Net Profit = $10,000 (10%) aka. Bottom Line

Tracking and Reporting

There are many different things that can be tracked and reported on. The more you grow the more you will want to track. For now we will focus on the main two types of accounting reports that you will need to get familiar with. These reports are the same reports banks are going to want to look at when doing any sort of loans. They are also going to be needed to extend your credit lines with vendors.

The profit and loss statement (P&L) is an accounting report that tracks numbers very similar to the example I just used. It summarizes the revenues, costs and expenses incurred on a particular job or within a particular time period. You can have a P&L for each individual job and you can have one for the overall company. I recommend reviewing both on a regular basis. The individual job P&L's will help you track the profitability of each job and help you make strategic decisions to improve on the bottom line per job. They should be reviewed weekly as jobs close out. The company P&L tracks the overall performance and profitability of the company and should be reviewed monthly, quarterly, annually, and any other time that would fit within the specific cycles of your business. Reviewing these reports regularly will help you pinpoint specific areas within your company to work on. Ultimately, the name of the game is to turn a profit.

The balance sheet tracks the overall health and wealth of the company. It summarizes the company's assets, liabilities and shareholders equity at any given point in time. It is used to determine how much your company is worth at any given time. This is where you will find all the company's debt or liabilities (credit card debts, bank loans, building and vehicle loans, etc.) and the company's wealth or assets (buildings, equipment, etc.). This report should also be reviewed monthly, quarterly, and annually. Viewing this report will help you build the overall value of your company and make it more attractive for investors and bankers in the future.

Accrual accounting tracks revenue and costs as they accrue regardless of what cash has exchanged hands. This method is commonly used in the construction industry because of the time it takes to perform the work that gets contracted. Work is conducted before all the cash is accounted for so we use this method for tracking projects.

Cash-based accounting tracks the revenue and cash flow in real time but it doesn't account for future work to be produced and closed. The revenues are recorded when cash is received and expenses when they are paid. This is not a recommended way to account for contracting companies but it is common way to file taxes because you don't want to pay taxes on money you haven't collected. It's important to understand both methods and use them as directed by your accountant. As I said before, I'm no accountant so it would be a good idea to sit with your accountant and have them explain all of this in further detail.

Job costing is the practice of tracking all the variable costs for each project on an individual basis. Job costing is very important in the contracting industry and can't be overemphasized. I'm surprised at how many companies in our industry don't practice job costing. They don't actually track the cost of every single job that they do. This is construction; there are many costs associated with each job. The main variable costs to track are labor and materials, but there are many other costs that can be tracked per job. Dump fees, fuel charges, commissions, project management hours, and equipment are a few. It's very important to track those costs so you can make decisions to ensure you are operating your business in a profitable way.

Of all the different types of small businesses, the construction business is one of the most complicated to account for because there are many different segments to track. You have booked revenue, i.e., jobs that have been booked but aren't built yet; production revenue, jobs that are booked and are currently being built; completed revenue, jobs that have been built but haven't been collected yet; and finally, closed revenue, jobs that have been completed and all income and expenses have been accounted for.

To make tracking all these segments more manageable, we've created a customized business tracking file. This file takes in CRM data in combination with data from Quickbooks to create tracking spreadsheets for all the different segments. It really helps track your numbers even though you aren't a CPA. For more information on getting a customized business tracking file or to see an example go to www.btacademy.com/SBGbook

It's very important to improve your understanding of your company's numbers to be able to make intelligent decisions that allow for increased growth and profitability. The more data you have, the more you know about it, the better decisions you can make. Tracking your numbers on a regular basis will increase your ability to make more micro changes to your business versus making macro or big drastic changes at the end of each year. It's much harder to turn a ship around than it is to change direction a few degrees.

Percentage-based tracking is a great way to make these micro decisions and to create budgets. I've learned the hard way that to run a good, sustainable growth business, you need to start tracking percentages. You want to know exactly what your average percentages are for all your fixed costs as well as your variable costs. By knowing what percentages you need to shoot for on each project you will be able to ensure that you bid on profitable jobs up front versus being surprised at the end. If you know what your average overhead cost is based on your average revenue, you can budget for new employees as you grow without affecting your bottom line.

Your accounting software will track all the main IRS and bank-required data, but there are still many other numbers that should be tracked and reported. These numbers include but are not limited to: leads, lead source, success ratio, and charge rates. There are a number of different software programs available that will track the information required by your company. These software programs are often referred to as customer resource management tools or CRMs. CRMs are designed to track each customer's project through the entire production process from when the phone rings to when the final check comes in. They can also be used to track and improve the customer experience. There are many programs to choose from, so make sure you choose the right one for you and your business. It's very important to have one of these software programs in place as early as you possibly can in your business. Switching CRMs after having an established business can be a daunting task.

Nearly all the things discussed in this chapter I learned the hard way. I did go to school, I took accounting and finance classes, I knew what revenue, net profit, gross profit, and net margins were. I knew the meaning of all these numbers, but I was so excited to start my construction company, that I forgot to pay attention to them. When I bid those first few jobs I didn't account for any changes or miscalculations and I didn't understand how to account for my overhead costs. That failure cost me dearly.

I soon found myself in a tough situation. I had lots of bills due and not enough profit to cover them. I couldn't pay for my trucks, my house or my personal expenses. I ended up having to borrow from Peter to pay Paul. I leveraged my good credit and put as much on credit as I could to try and salvage my company from complete implosion. The market was changing right under my nose and I didn't even realize it. I didn't have enough time to go sell new jobs because I was too busy trying to manage and work on my current ones. I didn't have enough money to pay people to do the work, so I was forced to do more and more of the work myself. The next thing I knew I had lost everything. I had to admit failure and defeat. I was faced with the biggest decision of my life... bankruptcy.

CHAPTER 4
It's Not What You Know...

Years ago, while working as a roofing salesman I was asked by the roofing company I was working with to go to Ohio to help them set up a new roofing operation where a recent hailstorm had happened. In other words, I was asked to go chase a hailstorm. They had set up a joint venture with a "local" Ohio based company that had no idea how to work a hailstorm. They basically paid to use that company's name. I had been subcontracted to work with the local company to sell roofs damaged by the storm. During my time there, I met a handful of storm chasers that had come from different parts of the country to work this hail storm.

I connected with one individual in particular that was a bit older than I and had been in the business much longer. I recognized right away that he knew what he was doing when it came to roofing sales and storm chasing. We connected right away and became friends. He had mentioned during the course of our conversations that he had made some good money in this industry. We connected well, so I tried to learn as much as I could from my new friend.

One night, about three weeks into this storm we were hanging out after a long day of door knocking. We happened to see on the news that Denver had gotten hit by baseball-sized hail. I figured if it was big enough to make the news in Ohio, it was big enough for me to go back home to work. At the time, I still had my own construction company registered back in Colorado. That company was essentially dormant at the time while I was off "chasing storms." I was subcontracting to this other company but my values and their values weren't aligned so it was only a matter of time before we were going to part ways.

It was at that moment it dawned on me that I could start my own roofing company. My new friend and I got to talking and I explained my company set up and my new idea to him. We had nothing else to do so we stayed up all night planning out this new roofing company idea. He had already been in the industry for a while and had some good insight for me. After getting our plan down on hotel notepaper we knew our next problem would be to secure funding.

I had no money at the time and was trying to recover from a bankruptcy. I figured that I needed about $100k to get started but I would take whatever I could to get. I knew I had no chance to get funding from a bank. I also knew that no one in my family had that kind of money so, I asked him. I figured, "What's the worst that could happen?" He actually challenged me to go raise at least $25k from someone else and when I did, he, in turn, would write me a $15k check as that's all he was willing to give me. I would then be able to start my roofing business with at least $40k cash. It was short of what I really needed, but I figured I could make up the rest as I went along. My mission was to find 25k. I packed my bags and left Ohio the very next day.

Mentorship

A mentor who can guide you and teach you from his or her own experience is a valuable tool to have in the business world. My new friend and first investor was definitely a mentor of mine and I learned a great deal about life, roofing and business from him. He was there for me when I first got started and helped me to get my roofing company off the ground. To this day, I still stay in touch with him.

However, he's not the only mentor I've had. Many of us have mentors in our lives that we may not even know we've had. We interact with new people everyday and don't pay attention to all the things we are learning. A lot of us have had fathers, family members, father figures, or teachers who mentor us. A mentor is anybody who knows something about something, and whom we trust and want to learn from. There are mentors all around us, and I encourage all entrepreneurs, especially in the construction industry, to find someone who knows more than you, and who will let you pick their brain, and try to learn as much as you possibly can.

A mentor is somebody that I look up to and whose knowledge, experience, and values I respect. Someone that I look to for guidance and can bounce ideas off of and someone that I can look to for honest feedback. It's important for you to decide what you want to look for in a mentor. One of the most important things I learned as a young entrepreneur was; if you surround yourself with successful people, you will become successful. It goes back the old saying, "If you're the smartest person in the room, you're in the wrong room."

Networking

Starting out I had no idea what organized networking was. I thought networking was just randomly meeting and connecting with people, or making friends. I didn't know how to network, or where to find a group of likeminded business people to network with. It was my roofing company's first supplier rep that first introduced me to networking. He invited me to be a guest at his networking group and I dove right in. Once I figured out what structured networking was, my business life changed completely. Networking was the biggest reason that I was able to get my business off the ground and onto an upward trajectory.

Networking is meeting and exchanging information with one person or with a group of individuals for the purpose of cultivating productive business relationships. Usually, networking takes place face to face, but with today's technology you can network with people all over the country, or even all over the world. There are many different organized networking groups, from chambers of commerce to small-industry-specific mastermind groups.

The networking group that I like the most is called Business Networking International. (www.bni.com) They meet weekly and are limited to one member per business category. There are chapters all over the world and each individual group has its own set meeting time which is strictly adhered to. They meet in the morning, afternoon, or sometimes over lunch. The hour to hour-and-a-half meetings give you the opportunity to build relationships with 20 to 50 other business owners and professionals who are in different industries than you. The objective of this type of group is that everybody works together to help build and grow each other's businesses.

There are many contractors that aren't aware this opportunity exists and they don't realize what an asset a networking group can be. When you get into a networking group, you're not going to automatically start getting more business. Business and networking it is all about building relationships. It's important to attend every week and put the effort in to build those relationships.

Once you get to know these people, you'll start to form what we call "power groups." Power groups are comprised of similar, corresponding industries that complement each other's businesses. An example of this would be a realtor, a mortgage lender, and an insurance agent. In the contracting and roofing industries, it's very important to network with realtors, insurance agents, solar companies, and general contractors who don't specialize in roofing. It's important to connect with these people because a good relationship is what drives people to confidently make recommendations and give you referrals.

In order to help create and/or be a member of an effective networking group, you must commit the time, be straightforward, and focus on building relationships within the group. Networking isn't all about you and how many leads you can get. You must do more than just show up; it's all about giving to others in order to eventually gain for yourself. To this day, my team is in multiple networking groups all over our state.

There are do's and don'ts when you are in a networking group. Here are a few things I learned that should help you make the most of your networking experience. Do give information, help others, show up on time, communicate when given leads, and show up looking professional representing your company in the best possible way. Don't talk about politics, give sales pitches (nobody wants to hear a sales pitch), show up late, not show up at all, or burn any bridges.

Strategic Business Partnerships

Another important piece in building your contracting or construction business is to create and maintain healthy business relationships with your manufacturers and your suppliers. Every sector of construction, whether it's siding, roofing, windows, gutters, foundations, concrete, building, or general contracting, has sub-contractors, manufacturers, and suppliers. Regardless of the area of construction you are specialized in, you have those three components. It's very important to have all three working in sync with one another.

You want to start by building a good solid relationship with your supplier. Your supplier is the key to your future growth and you will need to lean on them to increase your limits as you grow. It's a good idea to find a supplier that you trust. Learn who the rep is and make a point to get to know that person to build a good working relationship. When I failed and lost everything, I didn't have any supplier relationships. I had credit cards, and I had Home Depot which can only get you so far. Cash is not going to last long enough to sustain a growing business in the construction industry. When you're starting out, it's vital that you establish a line of credit with suppliers and you had better make your payments when they come due. Without suppliers, it's almost impossible to scale. You can have everything else in line; you can have the market demand; you can have the greatest installers in the world, but if you can't supply the materials to get the job done, you're stuck

Once you've established a relationship with the supplier you'll want to use that relationship to connect with manufacturer's. The manufacture is going to be a much larger company with a much larger marketing reach. Such a relationship can allow you to have a bigger, stronger brand by associating yourself with their, more recognized brand. Many manufacturers have contractor programs that put on trainings and seminars. It's a good idea to attend as many of those as possible. In most industry's, there are multiple big manufacturers available. It's a good idea to learn as much as you can about them, choose the one that best fits your business, and commit to doing business with that manufacturer. It will definitely help you grow and create longevity, credibility, and sustainability within your business.

The moral of this story is that it's not always about what you know about a particular industry or trade. It is more about what you can learn and whom you can learn it from. It's about who you know. You see, all businesses, not just the construction industry, are more about relationships than anything else. You never know what you are going to learn from the people you encounter each day and you never know whom you might meet that will change the course of your career. All you can do is build as many meaningful relationships as possible and learn as much as you can.

The day after I wrote my plan out on that hotel notebook, I drove back to Colorado with my mind set on finding that $25k. I started thinking about anybody and everybody that I knew who had some money who may have been in the construction industry. I wracked my brain trying to think who I knew and had a relationship with who I could approach for $25 grand. I had no clue how to do that. I proceeded to get the company started without having that piece in place yet. I was moving forward completely on faith.

It finally dawned on me that I had had a friend who had owned a big drywall company that we used when I worked for the general contractor a few years prior. I knew he had done well, and had built a good-sized drywall business. He had a big, badass truck and nice new house, so I thought of him. He had talked about starting a roofing company in the past so I knew he had an interest in the industry. He invited me to meet him at his home office. We hadn't seen each other in a few years and I was a nervous wreck. I had no other options at the time. I had to make this work. I arrived at his home and went downstairs in his office where I sat for what felt like an eternity and laid out my business plan. I was to turn my old construction company into a roofing company and we were going to make all the money. I even laid out what I thought the numbers were, and what I thought the return was going to be. After hours of discussion and selling my idea I ended up not only getting a $25k check, but he also added me onto his existing supplier account, which was a huge bonus since my credit was non-existent at the time.

The very next day, I took that check and I walked into my first investors office and put it on his desk. He couldn't believe it. He hadn't even thought that I might actually pull it off. Sure as heck, he opened up his checkbook and wrote me a check totalling $15,000.00. The moral of the story is that business and life are really all about who you know. If I had never gotten that first construction job I would have never met the person that eventually invested in my roofing company. You never know in life who you're going to meet and who might launch your life and career into a completely different direction. Business, really isn't all about what you know, it's about who you know.

CHAPTER 5
Building the Right Foundation

I remember the night when I came up with the idea and the business plan to start my own roofing company. I knew exactly what I wanted to do, and I made a list of things that needed to be accomplished. I had a plan but I didn't have people to execute that plan. It just so happened that my mom was unemployed at the time. I knew she had some previous experience with budgeting and bookkeeping. She always was really good with numbers; she even had me keep a budget at a young age. Therefore, it just kind of made sense to hire her. After all, I needed somebody that I could trust; someone to keep me in line, handle the budget part of the job, and make sure that all the money was being tracked properly. First, I had to convince her to quit what she was doing at the time, which was living as an in-house nanny for my sister and commit to working for me full time. She had already helped me manage things when I was selling roofs, but that was on a part-time basis. When I called and asked her to come work for me full time, she gave me one condition. Always keep your faith a top priority in your business and in your personal life. I agreed and fortunately, Mom believed in me and started working right away. Mom was employee number one.

Now we needed sales. I realized I needed a person in the sales management position that was a go-getter and an entrepreneurial-minded person that thought about business like I did. I called a good friend of mine who I knew from business school, where we had done a few business projects together. We previously had a roofing sales company, so it just made sense for me to ask him to be my sales manager and to help me with the new business. He agreed and off we went, selling roofs and trying to find more people to sell roofs for us.

5 Pillars of a Successful Trades Business

Since that time, I've learned a great deal about people and how to find the right people to build a foundation for a great business. I've created what I refer to as The Five Pillars of a Successful Trades Business. I definitely figured this out the hard way. These pillars are the five different positions that you need to fill in order to have the right foundation to scale your construction company.

This is a bit similar to an idea proposed by Michael E. Gerber in his books *The E-Myth* and *The E-Myth Revisited: Why Most Small Businesses Don't Work and What to Do About It*. In his books, Gerber describes three pillars of entrepreneurship and three types of personalities; the three types of people who you need in order to build a business. I, however, wanted to take that a step further. Based on my own experiences in the construction and roofing industry, I came up with five main components to laying the right foundation for a successful company.

The Carpenter. The first pillar, keep in mind we're talking about construction here, is the Carpenter, who, of course is skilled labor. This is the guy who knows exactly how to build what he's trying to build, he knows the specific tools needed, and is meticulous about his work area. The carpenter wants to complete the job as quickly and effectively as he can. He's an expert in his field, but more importantly, he is all about quality construction. Doing it right is the only thing that matters. This is your master carpenter and every construction company needs to have one.

The Manager. The second pillar is the Manager. This is a detail-oriented person. This is the person who wants a process in place to do a job in an orderly fashion. He or she appreciates structure in their daily job and wants to help build processes within the business structure. The manager is the person who is able to oversee other people, manage the construction process, and make fine tweaks to those processes as you build your business.

The Salesperson. The salesperson is the third pillar. This is arguably the most important position and could be listed first, but we are building a foundation here, not just flash-starting only through sales. This person is a go-getter. This is the person who wants to accomplish as much as possible while maximizing their time and getting their most profitable output for their effort. Salespeople are all about the money. They want to know what the profit is and how much of it they can make. They generally are free spirited and don't much care for paperwork and time clocks. They are interested in signing deals and getting money as quickly and easily as possible. This person is essential to any business; without sales you don't have a business.

The Bean Counter. The fourth pillar is the finance person or, the bean counter, whose importance can't be overemphasized. This is the person who watches the money; they count the beans going in and coming out of the business. This person is detail oriented and analyzes the data, analyzes the financials, and makes business decisions based on numbers, not gut feelings. He or she makes decisions based on what things are going to cost and not what the return is going to be. Often times, this person has a conservative approach to spending money and is always looking at ways to cut costs rather than increase expenses. That's the mindset of the bean counter.

The Entrepreneur. Last but not least, the entrepreneur is the fifth and most important pillar of all. The entrepreneur is necessary to build and develop a successful trades business. The entrepreneur is the visionary for the company. They have the big ideas—the big-picture vision that leads the charge. They want to take over the world. This person is often, but not always, the person who starts the company. A person with this type of personality is generally not very detail oriented, and one who thinks about the end result rather than the process and the steps necessary to achieve the desired result. This person is focused on the solution and not the problem at hand.

The important thing about these five pillars is that while each pillar is unique, they also correlate with one another in a number of ways. Think of the pillars not as job titles, but as personality traits. You're not going to just start a company and have 5 different jobs with titles right away. There are features of each one of these traits within each of us as business owners. Often times, our inner entrepreneur gets us to start a business, but we may not be a natural carpenter, bean counter, or manager. We may just be a natural-born salesman.

The majority of construction businesses or contracting trades companies are made up of one of two types of these pillars. First is the natural salesman, the person who has previously sold home improvement products, and who has most likely seen some success in sales previously. They eventually decide to open their own company. The second type of person likely to start his or her own trades business is the skilled carpenter. This is the guy who has spent years mastering the skills of the trade and the time has come to start their own company. The majority of construction companies are made up of either the carpenter or the salesmen. They are both entrepreneurs but they might not have the experience to be a leader and a visionary yet.

The trick here is to figure out how to learn the other four pillars duties, or find people who are naturally good at the ones you are not.

Starting out, both approaches can be difficult. Frequently, when you're starting out, you're building a foundation with just you and perhaps one or two other people. This may mean that you have to be the carpenter, manager, *and* salesman. You might have to be the entrepreneur and the bean counter when you first start a business. This is the place where you are wearing many hats, if not all the hats. How do you get past the hats? How do you get to a good foundation to get past the frustration of not being able to grow your company?

You can start removing the hats by asking yourself those self-awareness questions, as discussed previously. You will be able to rank your abilities from best to worst. You want to ask yourself which of the five fit your personality the best and which fit the worst. Rank them one through five. Once you determine your order of these five components, you want to start building your business backwards. Start finding people who complement your strengths while adding value to your weaknesses. Slowly work yourself to a place where you can focus solely on the things you are naturally really good at. You'll want to find people whose strengths complement what you are not as good at. Once you can get to that place, you will have a great foundation from which to start scaling your business.

To put in context what I'm trying to explain, building a business is a lot like building a house. It starts with a blueprint. You need to have a plan. You need to have a good idea of what you're doing and how you're going to do it. You first must dig a hole deep enough to pour a solid concrete foundation. Once you're done with the foundation, you build a frame. After the framing come the walls. These walls are there for support. Now, you can remove a wall, and the house is still going to stay up, but it's just not going to have the same rigidity; the walls are important, but they're not the base. You can't build a business or a house from the walls in. You have to build it from the ground up.

Once the walls are in place for support, the roof and the exterior get completed; things like shingles, siding, and paint get installed. These exterior coverings are not structural, but they do protect the house from external things that can cause damage internally. They protect the house they protect the business.

Finally, come the aesthetics. Aesthetics refers to the colors and all the finishes that make a house look beautiful and appealing to live in. These are the things that people see on the outside. Inside aesthetics can include cabinetry, flooring, lighting fixtures, and anything else that makes a house look beautiful. What you don't see is all the things underneath the pretty paint and flooring—the things that have to be in place before the pretty finished product can be shown.

The aesthetics are last for a reason. The aesthetics are what people see on the surface. At some point when you are building your business, you might find yourself comparing what your business is doing to what other businesses are doing. You may see other businesses that are really successful and doing great things; businesses that have great branding and great reputations, while you're still struggling. You might be trying to figure out how to reach that level of success. You can't compare the aesthetics of your business to the aesthetics of another. You don't know what kind of foundation that other business might have. They might have major financial issues or a very high turnover rate. The point is that you have to focus on building your house one step at a time—dig your hole, pour your foundation, build your walls, add the aesthetics at the end. You should be comparing yourself to yourself and focusing on getting better, not focusing on what others are doing. Eat the elephant one bite at a time and your business and your house will be strong.

Organizational Structure

An organization is a body of people with a particular purpose. An organizational structure is where each person's role, direct report and KPIs are created and illustrated. You will want to be mindful of growth as you design your company's organizational structure. It is important to have a structure in place early on, even if it's just one or two people. You will want to have an organizational chart and a list that describes what each position's duties and responsibilities are. You'll want to create a flow chart that looks like a pyramid starting with the CEO, flowing down into the other positions in order of responsibility within the company. It may have you (the CEO) followed by a sales manager, with a production manager next to the sales manager. When you have a full foundation, it will have you on top with 4 people on the same level or directly below you. It's a really good idea to look ahead when building your organizational structure. Try and visualize what your organizational structure is going to look like in one year, in three years, and five years from now. This will help you cast a vision for your company. Thinking about and planning for the future will help give you a roadmap and a destination to work toward. It will keep you on track to build that great home or that great business that you want to build.

In this organizational chart, you want some sort of title for yourself. I'm not big on corporate titles, so I like to get creative with them. You don't want a title that's boring or one that belittles someone else's title. I believe that every person in the company plays an important role in the success of that company. Everyone is on an equal playing field, they just have different responsibilities to fulfill. It's a good idea to create titles based on your industry that are unique to your company, sculture. You don't have to have a textbook type of a title. For instance, my title in my business is Chief Strategy Officer. I determined my biggest strength is strategizing and coming up with ideas. In *Strength Finder 2.0*, the quality is referred to as idealism and being a visionary. So, what do I do? I embrace that. That's how I came up with Chief Strategy Officer as my business title. I focus as much of my energy on growth and strategy for my company as I can. Some other examples are: naming a secretary an "administrative assistant" or titling a salesperson a "project manager" or "client relations manager"

```
                    ┌─────────────────────┐
                    │ Entrepreneur / CEO  │
                    │ Deliverable: Revenue│
                    │ and Profitability   │
                    └─────────────────────┘
```

Bean Counter/ CFO Deliverable: Manage Finances and Books	General Manager Deliverable: Manage Daily Operations	Sales Manager Deliverable: Generate Profitable Revenue	Carpenter / Production Mgr Deliverable: Build Quality Projects on Time on Budget
Invoicing Payroll Human Resources	Customer Service Admin Assistant	Marketing Sales Team Business Development	Production Assistant Service Repairs Installations

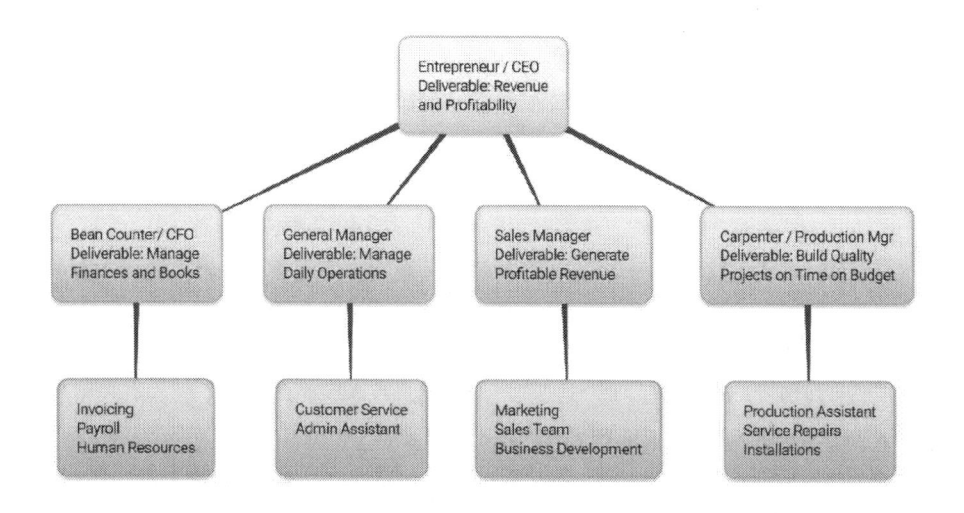

Duties and Responsibilities

All great companies have clearly defined duties and responsibilities for each position within the organization. From employee number one all the way up to employee number 100, it's very important to continually define and redefine duties and responsibilities as your company grows. As you add people, you'll need to add job descriptions. You will want to separate duties from existing employees to create the new positions and their responsibilities.

You'll next want to implement company procedures and systems. Company procedures are a predetermined way that your company conducts business. They are a set of guidelines for your staff to follow while doing their daily duties. A system is a set of principles according to which something gets completed. A system is a step-by-step way to execute "x," in order to execute "y," in order to execute "z." Having appropriate procedures and systems in place are crucial to any organization's success.

Systems and processes go hand in hand. A process is defined as a series of actions or steps taken to achieve a particular end. By applying systems and processes to your business, you are systematically working towards achieving your goals. This will help you on your journey to working on your business and not in your business. If you want to build a house, you have to have a process in place for that. You can't build the walls before the foundation. You can't do the foundation before you dig the holes, so you must have a process in place for everything. Many people in our industry fail because they don't pay enough attention to systems and processes. The more you can define your systems and refine your processes, the more effective, efficient, and profitable your company will become. If you can effectively build a system and a process, you can effectively duplicate that system and process.

At the time of my first two hires, I didn't know what personality assessment tests were or what they were for. I didn't know there were tests to measure a person's strengths, weaknesses, and personality traits. I just got lucky in a sense because I hired my mother, and she was very good at details. She became not only my manager, but since she was good with money, she was also the bean counter. I was able to fill two of those roles right off the bat. I know that I'm not that detail oriented, and I know I have a habit of spending money I shouldn't spend, but I was blessed to have a mother who could fill both those positions.

I was a third-generation carpenter and I had experience in building things. I had watched and helped my dad build many things growing up. I was good with my hands, so I could pick up some of the skilled labor duties or at least was knowledgeable enough to hire skilled craftsmen. I was also the entrepreneur. That was no doubt one of my strengths. I was a go-getter and good at sales, but no business can grow if one person is wearing too many hats.

I wasn't as fortunate with my second hire as I was with my first. My second employee was a college buddy of mine with whom I had worked on some business projects in the past. I thought it just made sense to hire him even though I didn't quite know where he was going to fit in the business. I figured that he could be my sales manager. I hired my buddy. I knew that we thought a lot alike, but what I didn't realize was in terms of pillars, he was a salesman, but also an entrepreneur. Therefore, we didn't exactly complement each other. I didn't assess what strengths and weaknesses he had compared with mine. Unfortunately, we had completely different mindsets on some key principles. My focus was on people and helping people grow and succeed. His focus was on himself and unfortunately, greed took over and that relationship ended in disaster. Employee number two was mistake number one.

Many of you are going to be able to relate to this. There are many contracting companies out there that hire family and friends. Working with family can be very difficult. It can also be very productive. I'm not suggesting that you refrain from hiring family or friends, but there's a proper way to do it. At this time, I have six family members working and have had up to eight working for my company. All our personal and working relationships are intact, but it wasn't always that way. We created a positive family environment by not requiring them to fill jobs just because the business needs a job filled. We were able to apply the same concepts from this chapter to put family members in positions that capitalized on their strengths and avoided their weaknesses. We try to find natural fits for their personalities. When we put family in a position to do something that they were naturally good at, they tend to enjoy their life and their job much better. This has helped us build a family culture that thrives together…most of the time.

Whether or not you build your foundation with family, it's important that you take your time to build it the right way. Think about your business foundation as a permanent fixture in your business. As you hire the key foundational pieces, make sure to hire people that have the same values as yourself and your business. You want these people to be in it for the long haul. You want to find people to help you build something great. It's not going to happen overnight but you will build a successful company much faster with the right foundation.

CHAPTER 6
Hiring the Right Team

I am both a huge sports fan and passionate about business. I've learned a great deal from sports that correlates to business and building the right business team. The Chicago Bulls with Michael Jordan won six championships in the 1990s. That team is known as one of the greatest dynasties of all time. How did they win six championships? Was it all because they had Michael Jordan on their team? It wasn't all because of Michael Jordan; they won six championships because they had a great system in place. Their coach, Phil Jackson, was known for his "triangle offense." He drafted great players with the right attitudes, taught them his system and worked extremely hard to master that system.

The New England Patriots are another good example. (Even if you don't like them!) The Patriots don't win championships every couple of years and aren't always in contention and always regarded as one of the top teams in the NFL just because they had great players. It's because they have a great system. It's because they adhere to a process that's been put in place by their coach, Bill Belichick. Process is everything, so all they do is they plug in good, talented players. Almost always, those players end up outperforming expectations because of the organization's process and system. Master the system and you will outperform expectations.

We took a similar approach when building out our business. We took the "field of dreams" approach: "If you build it, they will come." We focused our energies on building a company that sells itself. In doing so, we created a great company culture. If you as a business owner can focus your energies on creating a culture for your company and focus on building a company that sells itself, you will also build a great company. You accomplish this by mastering systems and processes, by hiring great people, and by building a great reputation. People want to be apart of something, so create an environment that people will want to be a part of. Having a great culture makes the recruiting and hiring process a lot easier.

A positive company culture is founded on core values. I learned this from my mom and dad. We were always taught to have good values and to put our faith first. When I launched my roofing company, we started with creating company values. We asked ourselves, "Why do we do what we do? What values do we have personally and how can these be incorporated within the company?" We started with instituting company values and tried to hire people who fit right into those company values. We didn't always get it right, but over time, we built a great company with a great culture that attracts great people.

I would encourage anyone starting out to ask themselves the same questions we did. Create your own set of values that you can build around, then lead by example. A company's culture is a direct reflection of that company's leadership, so be a great leader and put the right leadership in place first.

Personality Assessments

Once the values are established and the leadership is put into place, you can focus on the rest of the team. The next question is: How do I actually find the right type of people? One way to accomplish this is by having current employees and potential employees complete the DISC assessment tests. DISC is a behavior assessment tool that focuses on four behavioral traits: dominance, influence, steadiness, and conscientiousness. It is based on the theory of psychologist William Moulton Marston. Over the years, it has evolved into a test that has around 75 questions. By taking the test, you will essentially be able to figure out what personality type you have. You can figure out your top strengths and your top weaknesses. This information can be very humbling but can also be very useful in business. Many corporations use DISC to evaluate people when they hire them, but it is fairly uncommon in our industry. I'm not sure why our industry is so primitive, but I do know that it is a great way to build a great team focused on one another's strengths and not their weaknesses.

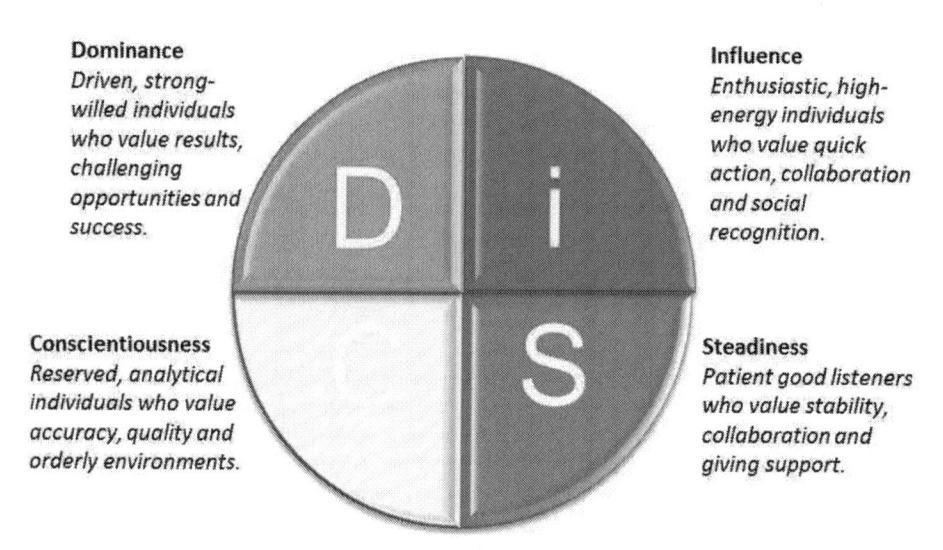

Dominance
Driven, strong-willed individuals who value results, challenging opportunities and success.

Influence
Enthusiastic, high-energy individuals who value quick action, collaboration and social recognition.

Conscientiousness
Reserved, analytical individuals who value accuracy, quality and orderly environments.

Steadiness
Patient good listeners who value stability, collaboration and giving support.

We didn't give our team DISC assessments until a couple years ago but when we did it changed our company. Upon completion of the DISC test, we were able to understand everyone's strengths and weaknesses much better. We were able to make changes to people's roles and job descriptions and were able to put them in better positions to thrive. When building your team it important that you do not try filling it with people who have the same strengths and weaknesses. You want a balance of people who will work well together to form a cohesive team. You want their strengths and weaknesses to complement one another.

Recruitment

Recruiting is one of the hottest topics in our industry. It's one of the most difficult things to do in the construction trades industry. Today, most people go online and place ads on Craigslist or some other media outlet or recruiting website. Back in the day, they ran ads in the classified section of the newspaper. The ads were usually brief, such as, "Experienced Carpenter Needed" or "Wanted. Salespeople." Not much detail was provided except a phone number or an address to send a resume. Traditionally, that was the way much of the hiring in our industry was done.

Another way people traditionally hire is through their personal network of friends and family. They may have a family member who needs a job, or they have a friend of a friend who needs a job. So, when a position opens, it's filled by a call to their friends and family. They don't actually do any assessment or analysis of what is needed; they just hire somebody just based on the position open at the time and the person's availability to start. Trust me, I know. I've made this mistake many times. I've learned that there are better ways to hire more efficiently.

Here's what I have learned about recruiting. It's not about fancy advertising or recruiting websites; it's about the people and the environment they work in. A different way to think about recruiting is, as I alluded to before, if you really focus your energy on building a company culture that creates an environment where people will enjoy where they work and want to come to work each day. They will naturally tell their friends and family about their job. Word will eventually spread to the public that you have a pretty good, if not great, company to work for. If you have a great company to work for and a new position opens up, you will be flooded with quality applicants. It's a lot easier to grow a happy team than a disgruntled one. To do recruiting right, you not only want to have a great place to work, but you want to back that up by having processes and systems in place for recruiting.

Start the recruiting process by analyzing the position that you're trying to fill. Don't start the recruiting process by calling your friends and family and neighbors. Actually sit down and write out exactly those characteristics, personality traits, and abilities required. We do this by filling out a form called the ideal candidate profile form. It helps you profile the ideal person who you want to work for your company before you start recruiting. Start with creating the profile, then you can use that profile to create a straightforward description and effective advertisement to attract the candidate you're looking for. You'll want to be straightforward on the job description and its difficulties. You should include your company's values and something that describes your culture. It's a good idea to start by sending your ad out to your company's email list and let them send it to their friends and family first. If that doesn't work, then you'll want to move to social media. Start with posting on each platform organically. You can actually pay to promote the ad if need be. Facebook is a great, inexpensive way to do this. You can also create a landing page to put on your website. We now have a career opportunities page on our sites.

A good salesperson is like gold to any construction company. Most owners have a hard time finding good salespeople. Applying all the things we just discussed will help you not only find good salespeople, but it will help you change your mindset about what a good salesperson is. If you don't have an extensive personal network or employee networks to tap into for recruiting, you can use search engine optimization to get your recruiting ad in front of the right people. You can create ads or pages on your website that directly target keywords that are commonly searched for by potential salespeople. It can cost money, but it's going to be more effective than throwing a boring ad on Craigslist like everyone else. You want to target people looking for a career in sales and not looking for a get-rich-quick sales job.

Interviewing

Having a good recruiting ad and finding good people is just the beginning of the process. The interview process comes next. What we traditionally do in our industry is, we either meet potential hires or salespeople at a bar, have a phone conversation, or we just bring them into the office and ask them some random questions to get to know them a little. From there, we make a decision totally based on our gut feeling. A much better way of interviewing ideal candidates for your business is to have a very defined interview process. Have a list of questions which pertain to the exact position that you're trying to fill and a clear idea of the abilities required.

Before you even set up an interview, ideally, you'd want to request each candidate to submit a resume for you to review. Unfortunately, in the contracting world, there are a number of applicants who may not have resumes. You don't want to completely limit your applicant pool with the resume requirement. Some quality workers aren't necessarily savvy enough to create resumes. When they do have a resume, it proves that they have a work history and the ability to operate a computer. It also indicates that the candidate has enough intelligence and experience to create an attractive resume, and that they value the position enough to present you with one.

Regardless of resume, you still want them to fill out a job application and they go through a standardized process. Next, you want to do a phone interview structured in such a way you can try to notice if there are any red flags that would eliminate this person from any further meetings. We call this initial phone conversation a conversion call. If you can have a good conversion call with some structure and organized questions, you'll save yourself a lot of time. You can eliminate candidates before you actually take the time to interview them.

Once you've done your initial conversion call with the applicant, it's important to conduct an in-office, in-person interview. The interview should be scheduled at a specified time and begin promptly on time. It's very important that you start the process off correctly; doing so establishes expectations of professionalism. If, for instance, the interviewee arrives at the appointed time and you make them wait 15 to 20 minutes before beginning the interview, that's automatically setting the precedent that you are an unorganized owner or an unorganized manager. If, on the other hand, the person arrives 10 to 15 minutes early, you start right on the dot, and handle it very professionally, the tone will be set for what should be a good employee relationship for many years to come.

During this interview, you want to have an agenda and have prepared a list of questions to ask. That list can be as short as a few questions to many questions depending on the position you're filling. If you're just hiring someone to answer phones, you're probably going to have a shorter list. Naturally, if you're hiring your new CEO or a new CFO for your company, your list of questions should be extensive. You can put your list of questions in a format that essentially allows you to grade them on the answers of each of the questions you ask.

Interview questions should be geared towards figuring out how the candidates abilities align with your company's needs and values. You want to find out about their abilities such as: [Tenacity- their ability to overcome challenges, Attainment- their preference for setting and hitting goals, Problem solving- their ability to find solutions to challenging situations, Precision- their attention to detail, and Leadership - their natural leadership tendencies.] You'll want to put some thought into creating questions that allow them the chance to give you a good evaluation of these attributes.

Once you've interviewed a handful of people for the same position and you've given each one of these candidates a grade, you can use the numbers to help make the decision for you. You're not just deciding based on your gut instincts, you're actually using an organized and structured process to hire the best candidate to help build and grow your business.

Onboarding

Onboarding is a term which refers to the process by which you bring a new employee into your organization. You should have a list of things that a new hire needs to do to become an employee of your company. It includes such basics as filling out paperwork and completing necessary tax documents, and receiving tools and materials to complete their job duties. It's important that the onboarding procedure should include a written employee agreement for every single employee in your organization.

An employee agreement is a document consisting of three to eight pages depending on the position. It defines the company's policies, procedures, and principles, and also specifies the employee's duties, responsibilities, and deliverables. A deliverable is the measurable task or assignment that the employee is required to complete on a daily basis. The employee should set goals based on their deliverables and they should get graded on these deliverables regularly.

It's important to have deliverables defined and acknowledged up front. Once you define duties, responsibilities, and create deliverables, you are now able to track and measure the performance of your employees. Being able to objectively measure performance is preferable to subjectively telling an employee he is doing a good (or bad) job. The objective measurement of your employees allows you to change and grow your business based on what you've learned through this process.

It's also a good idea to create employee manuals, even though very few businesses in our industry do. We're fairly primitive in that regard because our industry has many small businesses with very few employees. Whether you have ten, five, or three employees, you still want to have a manual detailing your company's standard operating procedures. It will make it possible to hire someone and immediately plug him or her into their new position within your company. You don't want to have to reinvent the wheel with each employee. By having a manual and procedures in place, you'll be in a better position to scale and grow your company at the rate that you want. Often, people are hired by a company and then they are thrown into the fire. They aren't given the tools and the training necessary to allow them to be successful. Many companies stall right here. When it comes to hiring, they don't have structure in place, which causes continual turnover. Construction companies are like revolving doors because they don't have the policies and procedures in place.

Manuals include what are called standard operating procedures (SOPs). Following a SOP ensures that one employee will perform a task or respond to a situation in the same manner that another employee does. You want to have a list of the jobs or tasks in your company and how they are to be completed. Procedures can include how to use your CRM to clock in or how to set up each jobsite. It's a good idea to maintain a list of exactly what to do and how to do it for as many jobs and procedures of your organization as you possibly can.

Employee Retention

Employee retention is an often-overlooked subject in many business operations. Employee surveys reveal that the number one positive thing that employees respond to in a business is not a raise and more money, it's recognition. The key to retaining employees is having a regular practice of employee recognition. When someone does a job particularly well, he or she appreciates being complimented. It's human nature. Most employees want to be recognized, and they want to be encouraged to do better. On the other hand, when an employee is doing something wrong or has made a mistake, instead of reprimanding and coming down on the person, look at it as a growth opportunity. The use of constructive criticism in teaching and training is more effective. Recognition is important and you want to continually reinforce your company culture. A company's culture is a direct reflection of the company's leadership. You as the leader and as a business owner must always be cognizant of the culture you're trying to build within your company. Look for daily opportunities on to reinforce that culture for your employees. You'll want to celebrate small and large achievements. Celebrate everything along the way.

As a leader intent on retaining employees, be transparent. If employees get the sense that you're hiding things, or you're doing shady business, they are not going to want to stick around. Employees don't want to support or follow a leader who isn't transparent. To a reasonable degree, let your employees know what you're working on and why you're doing it. When it comes to pay, you want to pay well, but not too much. You don't want to overpay, but you don't want to underpay either. To gain an understanding of the pay scale in your industry, you can do research online. If at all possible, you want to pay toward the upward end of the industry scale for that particular position.

Whenever possible, it's always a good idea to have incentive-based compensation. Give people a reason and the ability to earn above their base rate of pay. This not only gives people a sense of ownership and belonging in the company, but it is easier on you as an owner because you're not stressing out your overhead budget. Many times, you're rewarding an employee's exemplary performance which often directly correlates with an increase in the bottom line. Employees should be rewarded for doing activities which help grow your company and help your company increase profitability.

If you want to retain employees, make sure you take care of your people first. Don't flaunt your financial success; share it. Yes, you're an entrepreneur and a business owner and you're probably going to do very well financially. However, your employees don't want to see you driving up every day in a Ferrari, walking around yelling at everybody for mistakes and then taking off. They want support. Your employees want to know that even though you're making money, you have their best interests in mind. Remember to take care of your employees before you take care of yourself.

Reward your employees as a team with fun activities. Regardless of budget you should be able to find fun team building things to do outside of the office. Lunches and dinners go a long way. Set goals for the company and if your team hits those goals, reward everyone together. Have a retreat, a picnic, a great Christmas party, and do things that are going to create a fun environment amidst an often very stressful one.

When my partner and I planned our company, we took the same approach as some of the modern sports dynasties I alluded to earlier. The correlation is that if you build the system, find the right players, and focus on mastering the system, you can build your own championship winning team.

When we began, my partner and I wanted to build a roofing company that sells itself. To this day, we still focus on building a company that sells itself. We have built a company with a culture that reflects our values, and on that provides a fun working environment while providing for its employees and putting them first. It takes care of our customers at all costs and has the processes in place to not only hire great people, but to attract the cream of the crop. Build your team with the mindset that this is your time to win championships, not to just show up to the game. Business championships are won by hiring slow, firing fast, and by hiring character and teaching skills.

CHAPTER 7

Coaching, Training and Leadership

As a sports fan I watch nearly every major sporting event including the Super Bowl, NBA championship, college basketball championship, and golf majors. March Madness is my favorite time of year. I've followed some of the greatest players of all time: Michael Jordan in basketball and Tiger Woods in golf, and some of the great players in the NFL as well. What you can correlate between some of the greatest players in sports and the owners of successful businesses is… coaching.

Players such as Michael Jordan and Tiger Woods, for example, were talented without a doubt. But what separates the really great players from the rest is that they understand that they need to be coached to get better. Why is it that certain teams win more often than others? Is it because they just happen to have better players? No. It's because they have great coaching along with great systems as I discussed in the last chapter.

Consider the Green Bay Packers' history. They won the first two Super Bowls. It wasn't just because they had a great team or great players;

they had a great coach: Vince Lombardi. Lombardi was so great, in fact, that the Super Bowl trophy was named after him. The team was good, but it all started with great coaching.

Coaching

Coaching is one of the most important things to think about when trying to build your championship team in business. Start thinking about your business growth strategy. The objective is to get you to plan growth from a coaching perspective rather than from a management perspective. When you can embrace coaching as a managing style and embrace yourself as a coach and not just a manager, you'll be able to get in a position to achieve sustainable growth in your business.

Coaching is different from training in that it is the process of continually improving on a trained skill. The skill is trained when the employee is onboarded. Coaching is ongoing and is focused on growing and developing more skills. Coaching is done on a one-on-one basis and is essential in developing your key employees. A good practice of coaching your team will allow for personal growth and efficient company growth. You can hire the greatest people and you can build a great team within your business, but you must continually coach and mentor your team to create longevity.

Training

When hiring, you need to provide your team with the right tools to be a successful member of your organization. The right tools start with a well structured and effective training program. Small companies will not be able to have a training program in place right away; however, it's still a good idea to start building a training program piece by piece so you can have one ready when you get to a full growth stage. In the startup phase, you won't have all the systems and processes in place to train people on, but you can still find plenty of training and coaching programs to use for your team with minimal investment.

In all trades industries there are training programs available within each industry. Check with vendors and suppliers to see if they offer any training. You should take advantage of any free training program that you can. Even though you'll sometimes have to pay for it, there's no greater investment you can make than in training yourself and your team. When you invest in your employees, you provide the skills necessary for them to get better at their jobs and most importantly you create loyalty. The more education you can provide your team, the stronger your company will be.

Once you get to a place of scalability, or the growth phase, it's important to have your own training program in place along with training manuals. If people have training manuals, they will be able to learn their job duties faster and perform at a higher level. Provide tools for every employee to know what to do each day in order for them to work as effectively and efficiently as possible. Look at some of the greatest companies in any industry, not just the construction industry; one thing they have in common is great training programs. When scaling your business, you will want to start by determining what positions you will need to hire, how many people you will need, and at what time of year you will need to do it. Once you get your plan figured out then you will need to use a structured training program to execute that plan effectively.

To build an effective training program you will need 5 main components:

1. You will need an **orientation** in which the company policies and procedures will be explained. The orientation is a place to explain the purpose and the outcomes of the training as well as setting expectations for their daily responsibilities.

2. **In-office** training is training that can be done in a controlled environment. It can be at your office or at a rented space.

During this training, you want to focus on the specific tasks that the trainee will be doing out in the field.

3. After training your new employees as much as you can in the office, you will want to conduct **in-field** training. This training will be conducted on site and it should be conducted by the most experienced person on the team.

4. The trainee should be evaluated at each phase of their training. The purpose of the **evaluation** is to determine whether the trainee is ready to proceed with the next step in their training and ultimately to determine if they are ready to work out in the field.

5. Finally, there should be some kind of **team building** event that welcomes the new employees into your company while giving them a good sense of your company's culture.

Training should be an ongoing process; as your company grows so does your training program. You should always invest in continued education. This one isn't just for your staff; it's also for you. As an owner, you should always be looking for opportunities to continue your own education and gain leadership and management skills.

Accountability

With great coaching comes accountability. An effective coach is one who holds themselves and their team accountable. You can train an employee upon hiring them, and train them on a regular basis thereafter, but you also must have an infrastructure and process in place for accountability. One way to do this is by having employee meetings. I know we all hate meetings, but they are a necessary evil in business. You'll want to structure organized meetings with your team on a regular basis. Depending on your size and the growth phase you are in, you'll want to start with management meetings, then department meetings, etc. Meetings need to be structured with a specific agenda to avoid wasting time. I'm not telling you to spend all your time in meetings; I'm telling you to be very purposeful with the meetings you do have. The shorter the better.

All meetings should have an agenda or desired outcome. Many times, the desired outcome is that certain decisions are made or new changes are implemented. I can't structure your meetings for you, but I can tell you to plan and prepare for them. It's a good idea to start with at least a weekly and monthly meeting with your team and add more as your team grows. Each meeting should be interactive and every person should have a say in the desired outcome of the meeting. We like to set weekly goals in our weekly staff meetings. This helps give people a sense of accomplishment and keeps them accountable. A good rule of thumb is to open the meeting with positivity and close the meeting with positivity. Sandwich the negative stuff in between. Remember that people desire recognition. There should always be a recognition element to every meeting.

It is also important to have structured one-on-one coaching meetings with your staff. This gives you the chance to connect with and coach your key people and to promote and encourage personal development and growth. This also gives your team the opportunity to give you feedback. These meetings can be monthly or quarterly and should also include goal setting and recognition.

The key to retaining good employees is through structured hiring, onboarding, training, and coaching processes. Having these processes will allow you to build a culture of accountability within your organization. It's extremely hard to grow when you are constantly having to hire people to replace ones that leave. It is very costly to hire and onboard people. "What if I train somebody and they quit?" "What if I give them all this training and I teach them the job and then they decide to leave my company and start their own?" "It costs too much money to train people who are going to quit anyway, so why spend the money?" Don't worry about that because as long as you're running the company, you still want high level performers. Even if someone only performed at a high level six months after you trained them, you still had six months of a high-performing employee. And if they leave, they leave. Then you work on the process over again. You're better off having a trained employee for a short period of time than you are having an untrained employee for a long period of time.

Leadership

What is leadership? There are many interpretations of leadership and what makes a great leader. I study this all the time because I truly believe that every single company is a direct reflection of their leader. Leadership is all about inspiring others. I feel that great leaders inspire others to be leaders. It's extremely important that "you" as an owner, or the leader of your business, understand that everyone who works for you looks up to you in one way or another. Unfortunately, you will be expected to have all the answers. But you're not going to have them all right away. Therefore, you should make learning and growing a priority because it will reflect on your managers and on your staff. The better you can be as a leader, the more growth and success your company will enjoy.

Leadership starts with believing in yourself. Accept that you're not going to know everything. That's okay. Your staff isn't going to leave you just because you don't know something. They're going to leave you because you didn't acknowledge that you didn't know something, you told them something wrong, or worse, that you lied about it. That's what's going to get your staff to leave. Believe in yourself. Walk the walk. As a leader and as the manager of a company, act as if you do know. Lead by example. The harder you work and the smarter you work, the harder and the smarter your staff is going to work for you.

Another key point in leadership development is a concept referred to as servant leadership. I've read about this in a handful of different books. One I loved was called *How to Run Your Business by the "Book."* Servant leadership is important to me. I think a lot of managers and a lot of leaders, regardless of the industry they are in, tend to lead and manage with a mindset that they're the boss and everyone works for them. Without questioning, employees have to do what the boss says.

I want to challenge that. I believe that a great leader is a leader who has the mindset that the leader works for their people; that their people don't work for them. Here is a hypothetical example of servant leadership: There are two business tasks that are difficult, but need to be done. You have a manager to whom you want to delegate these tasks. How do you make the assignment? Are you better off walking up to that manager and telling him what he needs to do and telling him by when he needs to have it done? Or, is it a better situation to have a conversation explaining the two important tasks to him, letting him choose the one he wants to do and you offering to complete the other?

Which conversation do you think is going to have a better result? The one where you're just delegating and telling him what to do? Or the one where you're presenting the problem and letting him choose his own solution? That's an example of how great leaders have a mindset of serving others.

If you wake up every day thinking of ways to make your staff's lives easier and thinking of ways to create efficiencies for them, you're going to grow a really great company. You will demonstrate a mindset of servant leadership. You work for them, it's not the other way around.

My last advice on leadership is to remind you to personally and professionally reflect those qualities that we discussed in earlier chapters: honesty, integrity, and transparency. These are three key elements to being a great leader and getting your staff to support you. Instilling these values in your business culture goes a long way in creating a positive work environment. The absence of these qualities can cause a decline in efficiency because the employees don't respect the person they're working for.

Business Coaching

When it comes to leading your team to a business championship, you have to understand that you're not going to know everything. When asked, "What's one thing that helped me grow my company the most?" I respond with, "I swallowed my pride and partnered with a business coach." Today, I am a business coach. I coach other businesses and I have my own coaching platform. Yet, I still have my own business coach. Every two weeks, we meet to go over progress my company has made since our previous meeting, we examine what's likely happening in the future, and we set goals to push the growth of the business.

Not only do you want to think of yourself as a coach, It's a good idea to find your own coach. Even the Tiger Woods's and the Michael Jordans of the world had personal coaches; they didn't just have a head coach. They didn't just have Phil Jackson or Hank Haney to teach them. Michael Jordan had a shooting coach his whole career. Tiger Woods had a coach specifically to help him with his golf swing. It's a very good idea to have your own business coach as well. Even some of the greatest companies, such as Microsoft and Apple, hire consultants and coaches to come in and help their teams improve. It's a good investment to have a business coach to advise you on how to build and grow your company. The sooner you can get a business coach, the sooner you can overcome many of the obstacles created by not knowing what you don't know.

When looking for business coaches, there are many options out there. Many coaches work one on one and you pay per session or per hour. Essentially, they exchange their time for your money. Some have monthly fees that include a certain number of sessions available per month as well as pre-built programs you can have access to. There are many programs both online and offline out there for continued education in any industry. There are also many online education platforms coming available in the near future. I chose to partner with a coaching platform that has a number of coaches and different programs for construction trades companies of all sizes. They have a great business model and experienced coaches that provide great value to my company. The Breakthrough Academy works with many different trades companies and provides all the tools necessary to completely structure your trades business for profitability and sustainability. Whether your industry is roofing, painting, siding, gutters, general contracting, paving, or landscaping, the BTA has built a coaching platform that I highly recommend. For more information and examples on hiring, training and coaching go to www.btacademy.com/sbgbook

We have also built our own online training platform for roofing contractors that teaches contractors how to start, build, and grow their companies through a complete digital education series that teaches you step by step how to implement all the topics discussed in this book and much more. It includes seven modules with hours of video education that guides you through all your growth phases from startup to scalability. You can start, build, and grow your company at your own pace with *The Ultimate Roofing Startup Course* at www.theroofingacademy.com.

I know there are many choices when it comes to choosing a business coach or coaching program, so I would encourage you to find the coach or program that works best for you. The Breakthrough Academy works for established companies that have a desire to grow and the ability to work in a structured program with live coaching. The Start-Up Program at the Roofing Academy works for the company starting out that wants to work at their own pace. Regardless of what coach you work with, you will be able to get better and better at becoming a coach for your own team just by having your own coach to learn from.

I spoke about my passion for sports earlier and how the great individual players have personal coaches. Team performance is reflective of great coaching as well. One of my favorite sporting events each year is March Madness. I just love the rivalry, the competitiveness, and the amazing energy that comes with the NCAA tournament every year. Every year, a handful of the same teams always seem to be in contention to win. The reason for that is that these teams have great coaching and leadership. Some of the greatest college basketball coaches of all time, such as Roy Williams of North Carolina, Tom Izzo of Michigan State, and Mike Krzyzewski of Duke, are consistently in the mix with 28 combined Final Fours and 9 Championships between them. Why is that? It's because they understand what it takes to be a great leader. They lead their teams to victory by not only being a great coach and leader, but by being a mentor to these young players as well. They lead their teams to success and their teams follow them to championships.

CHAPTER 8

Building a Sales Program

When I first started in sales, I was handed a stack of contracts and a handful of papers that had some basic information about the company. I was told to go sell roofs. I took those papers and made a makeshift pitch book, and I went and knocked on doors. That was it. I had virtually no experience with sales and no formal training. I just jumped into the fire and attempted to sell roofs on natural ability. Although I was naturally outgoing and became good at sales, I had no real structure to my process.

When I started my own roofing company I tried to get a little more sophisticated with my process so I created a new professionally made pitchbook to use. I also knew I couldn't grow my company with my sales efforts alone. I needed more salespeople. I didn't really have a plan so I hired some buddies of mine by convincing them of the great potential of my new business. I gave them my new pitchbook and did my best to teach them what I knew but I didn't provide them the real sales tools they needed. I figured that some of them would be able to sell.

When that didn't work out, I tried hiring guys that already had experience. I figured that if they already knew how to sell and had experience I wouldn't have to train them as much. I was a small company just getting started. I thought that I would pay more commission than my competitors and that would help me get better, more experienced salesmen. I gave them the same tools I had. "Here's a pitchbook. Here's a contract. Go knock doors and sell roofs"

The Consumer

Unfortunately, too many companies either start out with this shotgun approach, or are still in this sort of mindset. Sales, in its simplest form, is the process of understanding a client's needs and aligning your products or services to what those needs are. We need to change our mindset to build a sales program the right way. We need to start thinking more about the thought process behind buying. Why do people purchase what they do? Why do people buy? Sometimes it has to do with something they absolutely need; sometimes they just want it.

When buying from a salesperson, people make the decision to buy for all sorts of reasons. Some buy from you just because you have a good personality, or you have a good haircut, or your breath smells good. One of the biggest reasons people buy a product or service is because the salesperson truly understands their needs. If a salesperson can make a good impression and provide the right solution for their client's needs, they will have a much better chance at selling their product or service.

Does your company provide a solution to client's needs, rather than just information? Do customers see value in your price? People purchase because of perceived value, not price. That is one of the most misconceived sales mantras in the industry. So many people are focused on price. They think consumers buy on price. They think they have to offer the lowest price in order to get somebody to buy. But in reality, people aren't buying on price. They're buying on value. They want to feel as if they got the best deal, and the best value for the money they've spent.

When are clients ready to buy? Who knows? People are ready to buy when mentally they're convinced that they need the product or that the solution to their needs is being provided.

How do they buy? It's pretty simple. Sometimes they sign a contract, sometimes the buy with the swipe of a credit card. A purchase at Walmart is completed with the swipe of a credit card. When you're buying a big construction project, a roof, or a new house, a whole different purchasing process is involved. Depending on the industry you're in, you must understand the particular needs of your consumer and why they buy in order to find the best solution for them. Building out a great buying process helps you sell at the highest, most effective, and efficient level possible.

The Sales Person

Sales people tend have their own agenda. Most salesmen are just looking to see how much money they can make with as little effort as possible. They want to get as many sales as they can and make as much money as they can in order to live the elaborate life that they want to live. Salesmen are naturally going to be a little bit greedy. That's not necessarily a bad thing. You need to be a little bit greedy to be successful because you have to be hungry. Greed is a double edged sword. Too much greed can ruin a person.

Salesmen of this type also want to control the sale's situation. They prefer to talk at the customer rather than to listen to the customer. They may try to push a sale onto the client. They're going to be focused, naturally, on their own needs—selling to a customer—instead of telling the client what they need to know.

This type of sales mindset is a thing of the past. If you want to build a successful business, you have to get that type of sales mentality completely out of your mind, completely out of your program, and completely out of the minds of your sales team. We're not here "just" to sell. Unfortunately, in our industry, a lot of people view construction sales, roofing sales, siding sales, or any other type of home improvement sales similar to the way they see used car salesmen. We need to change that. We need to erase that mindset completely. We are not used car salesmen.

When it comes to sales, I like to think of myself as an educator, not a salesman. I also see myself as a professional consultant, if you will. You're consulting with your client to provide a solution to their problem. The educator is going to ask questions about the client. He will take the time to get to know the client on a personal level and try and find a personal connection to the client. Do they like the same sports team? Did they notice a bumper sticker on their car that they can relate to? Do they have a dog? Do they both like golfing? If possible, they want to find a common interest. They actually listen to what the client's interests and needs are.

The Sales Process

Once you've established what the clients needs are, and advised about possible solutions to clients' issues, to close that deal you want to educate the homeowner on your company's process. People want to understand the process, especially when it comes to construction. If you can explain the process to a homeowner in a way that makes sense to them, you're going to have much better success in closing. It's all about explaining the process of the construction services that you're selling and how you're going to help them achieve their desired outcome. You're creating the value that ultimately builds the trust that you need to have between your client and yourself in order to close the deal. But you should understand that your company needs to have that process in place to be able to provide the right tools to help you and your sales team sell more effectively.

It's a great idea to build a sales process that can be taught, practiced, and duplicated. Over the many years I've been in this industry, I've been in many different sales situations and have learned many things the hard way. You should be able to learn something from every sales situation whether you close it or not. If you walk away from a deal that you don't close and you don't know why, you've completely wasted your time. If you know why you didn't get the deal, you can at least learn what not to do next time. The same concept applies to the deals that do close. If you close it and you don't know why you closed it, you're not actually getting better at sales. Over the years, I have studied and practiced many different sales systems. We have taken all the personal lessons we learned through experience and the positives of each sales system to build out a proven sales process that works.

To understand the sales process or to create or implement a sales system, you have to start by understanding the concept of Pareto's Law, or the 80/20 rule. It states "that for many events, roughly 80% of the effects come from 20% of the causes." In sales terms, that means that 80% of your sales volume will come from 20% of your salespeople. It also means that 80% of each person's outcome results from 20% of their efforts. For instance, 20% of the salesperson's time roughly accounts for 80% of their actual productivity. They spend 20% of their time selling deals whereas they naturally spend 80% of their time doing all the other things that go along with the sale.

Let's apply this principle to the sales process. First you need to illustrate the actual sales process, then you'll want to figure out which parts of that process lead to the highest amount of return. Example: You have 5 steps written out for your sales process: set up the appointment, inspect the project, write up the estimate, present the estimate, and close the deal. Using this 80/20 principle, you know that 1 of those 5 steps will provide 80% of the outcome. One fifth = 20%. The desired outcome here is getting a signed contract. The step that I would focus on the most is presenting the estimate. You will want to spend as much time presenting estimates as possible and as little time doing the rest of the steps as possible to get the highest overall outcome, that is, the most signed contracts.

This same principle can be applied to many different facets of life and business. This can also be applied to your sales team. If you have 10 sales people, it's likely that 2 of them account for 80% of your sales. The 80/20 rule is not an exact science, but it's a great way to get your mind thinking in a different way. If you first understand this principle, then you can make better decisions that lead to more efficient outcomes. To challenge this rule and get to a place where all members of your company's sales team are performing at a high level, you have to focus on the 20% activities. Build a sales process and system with the focus of mastering the important 20% of their activities and minimizing or delegating the rest of the less important tasks. Our sales system is based on these principles and we apply this principle to as many facets of life as we can.

Building a High Performing Sales Team

As discussed in an earlier chapter, it begins with building a company that sells itself. Focus your energy on building a company that sells itself, and it is much easier to train your sales team to close at a very high rate. As a part of a sales system, you'll need to provide your team with the tools necessary for them to perform at a high level. Too many owners hire salespeople without giving them any sort of tools, training, or system and they wonder why they aren't getting good results. We tend to hire people with experience, who might have worked for their competitors, or have been in the industry before. Who's to say that they were ever properly trained in the first place? It harder to break old habits than it is to create new ones. You've just created a situation that is even more difficult to get past. Rogue salespeople will do whatever they want, telling your clients whatever they feel will help them get the deal, not what is important to you and your brand image. You can't just rely on people with good personalities to sell your company's services at a high level. You need to be able to provide a great brand, materials, training, and coaching in order to build a high-performing sales team.

When it comes to attracting and hiring quality salespeople, you can use the same principles I discussed in the previous chapter. Create unique ads with a direct and honest description of the sales job, use your personal and employee network first, then start placing your ads on media outlets that cater to your target demographic. Conduct a phone interview before you conduct an in-person interview. Make sure to hire people whose strengths cater to the duties of your company's sales requirements. When it comes to sales, it's a good idea to hire people with the right attitude and personality over experience. Hire character train skills.

Once you've hired your first salespeople, it's important that you provide them with the right training to do their job. A good sales system includes ongoing training, and measures of accountability.. Many of the "sales tools" used today involve technology. We are in the age of technology and it's not going anywhere. If you're trying to provide in-home sales without using technology, you are way behind the eight ball. It used to be clipboards and pitch books; now it's laptops, tablets, PowerPoint presentations, automated emails, and videos that are selling the projects for you. Believe it or not, the construction industry as a whole is still living in the past. The more tools that you can provide your sales team with, the more you will differentiate your company; the more you will separate yourself from the old school contractors you are competing against. Your use of technology will also create excitement and efficiency within your team. The more your sales team is excited to work for your company, the more success they will have, which ultimately leads to more success for you.

The 7 Step Sales System

It's very important to have a sales system in place if you want to grow your company effectively. There are a number of age-old sales programs and systems kicking around every industry. Many industries have some sort of thought leader or sales trainer who you might be able to hire or purchase access to their system. You could spend as little as a few dollars to subscribe and learn online or up to a substantial amount of money for having someone else build out a custom sales process for you. After trying and studying many of these different programs, we decided to create our own. I believe that each company has unique qualities that make them different and that they should incorporate the things that make them different as a focal point of their sales system.

Most structured sales systems have somewhere between 7 and 10 steps depending on the industry and the type of product or service they're selling. The system that we have developed for our company is a 7-step system. We have created 7 simple steps that can be learned, practiced, duplicated, and perfected. This system can be applied to many different types of home improvement contractors and modified to meet the specific models within each industry.

1. The Set-Up
2. The Warm-Up
3. The Inspection
4. The Story
5. The Process
6. The Close
7. The Follow-Up

We have narrowed our process down to seven steps that, when executed properly, will greatly improve your sales team's performance on many levels. We have seen our team's closing percentages rise from 40% to 70%. But closing percentages are just part of the process. Most sales systems focus too much on the closing percentages and not enough time on the process itself. Part of that process is tracking and accountability. Our system has also increased the overall level of involvement of the whole team, it has increased camaraderie and teamwork, and it holds everyone on the team publicly accountable. Best of all, it has created a competitive environment with a very productive and efficient sales team.

My main bread and butter in business has been in the roofing industry. However, the processes and the structure of our system can be implemented in any contractor trades company. Remember, each company is unique regardless of the industry it is in. It's all about the process and telling your story. The reason for having a structured sales system in place is to set yourself apart from your competition while adding value to your company. This will help take price out of consideration when people are buying your services. This sales system is designed to accomplish just that.

The following breakdown of our 7-step process is based on my roofing company and has been built out over several years. The system may change as our industries are always changing and as technology improves, but the principles remain the same. Our goal is to take our prospective clients on a 7-step journey to build a relationship and to provide them with the solutions they are looking for while providing a great experience during that journey. And we TRACK EVERYTHING along the way!

Step One: The Set-Up

Every successful sale starts with a proper set-up. The set-up starts when the phone rings and moves to step 2 when the salesperson is at the house in person with the prospective clients. Whether you're knocking doors or you're running leads, it's important to set yourself up for the best chance of getting a deal as possible. When you are first starting out, you might be the one answering the incoming calls. I'd highly recommend getting someone to answer phones as quickly as possible. The first impression is important. When someone calls your company to inquire about your services, that is an opportunity for your company to make a sale and earn revenue. Every one of those calls should be treated like gold. You won't know how they heard about your company, but that is one of the first questions you or your office assistant should be asking.

The initial call is the first phase of step 1. There should be a specific way the phone should be answered each time. Every client should receive similar treatment throughout the whole process. You'll want to provide a short-scripted dialogue that your assistant can use to answer the phone each time. Keep it pleasant and simple. For example: "Thanks for choosing ABC construction. How can I help you today?" You should also provide a list of questions to ask your new customer. "How did you hear about us? What type of services are you looking for? What is your existing property like?" Base it on your services, i.e., What type of roof do you have?" In the case of roofing we ask how old, tall, and steep the roof is you can also ask if they have any storm or other type of damage. For restoration companies, you can ask if they have storm or other insurance related damage. The objective is try and figure out what their problem is ahead of time. Keep the questions simple and try and make them pertinent to your specific services. Make sure your assistant has common knowledge about the services your company provides. They should at least have an understanding of your production process, estimating and billing process, and common terms. Once the initial call is complete and all the necessary customer info is gathered, then you can set-up the appointment.

Phase 2 is the set-up call. The appointment can be set by an assistant right then and there, or the lead can be sent to the salesperson to call and set up the appointment themselves. I would prefer having an assistant to set the appointments up but it doesn't always work out that way, especially early on. During the setup call, it is important to let the prospective clients know what to expect during their inspection. Set the expectations for the time the whole inspection and/or estimate will take. Give them a brief description of what the inspector/salesperson will be doing, such as walking around the entire exterior of the house or inspecting the attic or basement.

Most importantly, make sure that the appointment is set at a time when both decision makers are there at the same time. Making sure all decision makers are present during your presentation will double your chances of success and will eliminate the "I need to talk to my wife" rebuttal. There are strategic ways to get to an appointment time that ensures all parties will be present without being too *salesy*. You can ask questions about the times and days they work and about their kids dance schedules, etc. to narrow down a few options that work. If they both work days and get home around six and their kids have dance on Tuesdays and Thursdays, you might want to offer times on Monday and Wednesday at 6:30. Give them a chance to get home but not a chance to settle in. Once they have kicked their feet up and turned on the game, they aren't going to be interested in what you are selling. Thirty minutes is ideal. The key here is to end the call with a confirmed appointment time and date set.

Phase 3 is the pre-appointment follow-up phase. This phase is intended to confirm the appointment and remind everyone about the date and time again. This can be done with a follow up phone call and/or email. In addition to the confirmation call, it's a good idea to give the customer a call when you are on your way regardless of tardiness. Whether you are late or not, you should call your customer as you are headed their way. This will reinforce your level of communication and professionalism while making sure that they didn't "forget about it" or need to "reschedule" last minute. This will help you avoid unnecessary trips. Windshield time is not profitable. The objective of the set-up phase is to prequalify your clients to make sure they are a good fit for you and your services and to get them into a committed appointment.

Step 2: The Warm-Up

Upon arrival you will start step 2, the warm-up. This step is intended to find commonalities with your prospective clients and get to know them a little. It is not about selling anything. The idea here is to talk about anything but the construction project or service you are trying to sell. It starts when you pull up in front of the house. It's a good idea to park in a visible place where everyone can see your clean truck and its company branding. Don't park in their driveway if possible and definitely don't leak oil anywhere. When you are walking up, it's a great idea to observe as much about the person as possible based on their property. What type of vehicle do they drive? Do they have any specific bumper stickers? Are there any sports team logos anywhere? Is their yard super clean or is it unkept? These observations can be very helpful when trying to find common ground with them.

When you open dialogue with your new clients, they are going to naturally have a barrier built up in their mind. After all, you are a salesman. This phase can last a few seconds or an hour. Be careful not to stay here too long. You won't have any time left to pitch. It's a good idea to ask questions and direct the conversation based on their answers. There will be a point during the conversation when you will need to switch it back to business. This takes a bit of practice to master, but usually it is when there is a break in topic or a gap in dialogue. When you switch from talking about their favorite car brand to their favorite sports team might be a good time to redirect back to business. The objective here is to make a genuine good impression and find some common ground with your client in order to lower their wall of apprehension. You want to switch from a "salesman" to an "educator."

Transition

Between each step is a transition and the transition between step 2 and 3 takes place when you switch back to business and start explaining the inspection process. During this step, you want to start asking questions about their upcoming project. You will want to find out things like whether or not they have other bids, is it an insurance claim, and what kind of budget they might have. You'll want to be specific with the questions you ask so as to not be too intrusive. The more information, the better. It's very important to ask them how long they have been thinking about their project because it will help combat the "I have to think about it" rebuttal later.

During the transition you want to set the homeowners expectations by explaining what all is going to take place over the next half hour or hour. Explain to them exactly what you will be looking at and what you will be looking for. Let them know that you will be presenting them with your findings and will be preparing a short presentation for them. The objective here is to set the tone for the appointment and establish yourself as the "expert"

Step 3: The Inspection

There are three parts to the inspection step: the inspection, the estimate, and the presentation set-up. During this step, you will begin by inspecting the project in a professional manner. This is also a good time to gather more information about this project. You can invite the client along for the inspection or inspect the project on your own based on your specific service. If you're doing a basement finish, you'll want them to show you exactly what they want to have done. If you're inspecting a roof or attic, you will most likely be doing the inspection on your own.

When doing inspections on your own, you will want to document any issues or problems you find. Most people just take photos and show them to their clients but we have gone a step further and started taking videos. We have a specific way to take a narrated video that highlights three areas of each project that need to be addressed. This is a great way to separate yourself from the crowd while providing added value to your clients. Be specific with your videos; don't make them longer than two minutes, and be safe while making them. It also a good idea to use a laptop or tablet to present the video. You will also be wanting to take all necessary measurements to create the estimate for your clients.

I won't spend a huge amount of time here on estimating as many different construction companies estimate things different ways. There are also many roofing contractors who might not be creating estimates up front. You will want to create and input your company's estimating procedure into the system in this step. One key to this part of the process is the "act" of writing an estimate. Whether you are writing a physical estimate or not, you will want to give yourself a few minutes away from your customer.

During this time, you want to set up your "presentation" and you want to give them the opportunity to do some research on your company. You can present them with a handout with company info on it for them to read. You can also present them with a previous client list for them to physically call your references. This is a great method but is not always the easiest to get accomplished. We prefer to direct them to our website if possible and to our online reviews. You can actually now get digital business cards that have all the links you want sent directly to the client's phone or inbox. You can simply ask the client for their cell or email and send them directly to your reviews, company site, or company promo videos. Customize it as you see fit. This is an unintrusive way of establishing credibility and turning a sales call into a referral call.

At this point you'll let the client know that you will be taking a few minutes to go "write the estimate" and you would ask them a favor. You can ask for their opinion on your new website layout or say, "Check out this new technology." Then you send them your links and say something like, "If you don't mind, I sent you some info on our company. Would you mind taking a look at it while I work up your numbers?" You can also come up with an incentive here. " If you call our references or check our reviews, I'll give you a free upgrade or $50 off your project".

Traditionally we have not even had a "presentation" with our prospective clients. We just give them some random company info along with an estimate. Then we go about our business waiting for them to call us back. When I started out I was given a 3-ring binder with some random company info and I was told to go sell. This was called a "pitch book." The age of the "pitch book" is over. This is the age of technology. You will want to have a digital presentation to complete the next 2 steps in this sales process. We use an interactive PowerPoint presentation that helps our team provide the same information to every customer. While writing your estimate, you will also want to set up your presentation by having the tablet or laptop already open to your presentation and logged in to wifi if necessary. The main objective at the end of this step is to get to the kitchen table with both homeowners ready to see your presentation.

Step 4: The Story

People don't buy from statistics and numbers, they buy from people. Every person and every company has a story. The objective of this step is to tell your story and your company's story in a way that humanizes yourself and your company. Telling a good story will help your client find commonality with you and your company. It will also help lower their apprehension barriers to a level where you can work towards a close.

The presentation should open with your story. Tell a story of how you got into this industry and why you chose to work for the company you work for. Everyone has a story to tell; use that story to build relationships. Use your story to be real and treat every sale as an opportunity to build a friendship. This will help you get to the other side of the table, so to speak. If they know why you chose your company, they can start to find their own reasons to choose that same company. You're not selling anymore; you're referring business to a company you trust.

After you tell your story you will want to use the presentation to tell the companies story. Remember your company's *why* and core principles. Start there and include other pertinent things like time in business, locally owned, or family operated. Be sure to promote any industry certifications and partnerships to give your company industry-wide credibility. You will also want to include any company achievements that are important to your story such as community involvement. Giving back is an important part of our company. We emphasize our partnerships with many different nonprofits. We even allow our clients to pick the nonprofit of their choice for us to donate to on their behalf. They also have the option to pick from a list that we provide. Telling a good honest story builds credibility both for your salesperson and your company. Once you've established credibility and piqued their interest in your company, then it's time to transition to explaining the process.

Step 5: The Process:

Step 5 is the step in which we want to educate our customers on the complete process of how their project is going to be completed. Again, each company has a slightly different process for how they produce their services. It is important to document that process in a way that can be easily explained by your sales team and easily executed by your production team.

Break your process down based on your business model and create presentation slides to illustrate that process. There may be more than one process to explain based on your industry. To get started, you can simply take pictures of a current project at each phase of the process. In the case of roofing, we start with material delivery and end with a final walk-through with a rolling magnet. We show pictures of each phase of the roofing project and our salesperson explains each phase throughout the slides.

You should also include an explanation of how the project is going to be constructed. We use this time to physically show our clients samples of the materials that they can choose from to get their project completed. We like to reconstruct all the components on a roof and let the customer physically touch each item. This is a good way to sell to more senses than just sight and sound. This is also a good way to break up the PowerPoint presentation while getting the clients interested in choosing their materials or picking colors.

It's a good idea to present upgrade ideas at this point. It's easier to adjust the type of product to lower the price than it is to try and increase the price after the fact. I always like to try to get the clients committed to a color or specific style at this point. The fewer the options, the better the chance of getting a color or material commitment. Present them with choices in a good/better/best format, be concise and limited on the variety. For example: you don't want to give a client 4 different manufacturers to choose from with multiple colors per manufacturer. You're better off giving them the good, better, and best options with 1 manufacturer that you know is one of the best options. It goes back to building strategic manufacturing partnerships. Many times, people don't know what they like until you point it out to them.

The final element to the process step is to explain the billing, or in the case of insurance restoration contractors, the supplementing process. If you are selling a retail product such as a new deck or new exterior paint job, you will want to explain how the billing works within each step of that process. If you don't collect money until you are finished, explain that. If you take a deposit when materials arrive and collect the final amount upon passing an inspection, explain it. It's important to set the expectations with your homeowners up front to avoid any delays in getting paid. Getting paid is the whole point of business.

Explaining the insurance process is one of the most important steps for restoration contractors who deal with insurance proceeds. Insurance projects can be very lucrative and profitable, but they can also be very complicated and it can take a long time to complete the entire billing cycle. It's important to explain this process to homeowners in a way that makes sense. Insurance claim paperwork can be difficult to understand yourself, let alone explaining it to someone else. This is best done visually and we have a whole module of virtual training on this subject online at www.theroofingacademy.com

The basics include understanding the terminology. RCV is replacement cost value. This is the grand total of what your project is worth in today's market prices: what it costs to get materials, pay taxes, and pay labor while maintaining a fair margin. ACV is actual cash value. This is the value of your project when it was completed without considering depreciation. ACV is also based on the expected life of that particular material and is calculated by dividing the expected number of years by the actual number of years since the material was first installed. Depreciation is the difference between the two. RCV - ACV = depreciation. For example, if a roof was installed 10 years ago and its life expectancy is 30 years, 10/30= 33%. The adjuster would depreciate the RCV by 33% to come up with the initial ACV payment: 67% of the full RCV.

Example: Assume this is a $10,000.00 RCV and the depreciation is 35%. 10,000 * .35= $3,500. $10,000 (RCV) - $3500 (depreciation) = $6,500 (ACV).

The last main term that you will want to know is the deductible. The deductible is a predetermined figure that the homeowner has contractually agreed to pay in the event of an insurance claim. Deductibles can be written in the policy different ways by different insurance carriers. The two most common deductibles that we see are either a predetermined dollar amount, $500 or $1000, or they are the equivalent of a small percentage of the value of the property. One percent of a $300,000 property equals $3,000.

As you see, this is a complicated process that changes rapidly. We spend more time mastering this step than any other when we are selling insurance-based projects. Regardless of your business model, it is very important to first develop a process for everything, then explain that process to your potential clients. Not only will you come off more professional than the competition, you might actually be able to perform it the way you sell it. The purpose of this step is to explain everything, answer all the clients' questions, and answer as many potential rebuttals as possible before they are given. By explaining your process to your homeowner, you are working towards setting up your close.

Step 6: The Close

The close consists of two parts: the pre-close and the "close close." When you get to a point in your presentation when it time to start talking numbers, you will be ready for the pre-close. The purpose of the pre-close is to try to eliminate rebuttals that have nothing to do with the price. Before you give your clients a price or ask for the sale, you want to make sure that you have answered all their project-related questions. This way, they can't revert back to the project or deflect when you give them the price. When I first learned about pre-closing, I learned it a very specific way. We would ask, "Other than price or payments, would there be any reason we couldn't get your job started today?" That statement makes a lot of sense because it is a soft way of saying, "Can I have your business if price wasn't a consideration?" This type of question should give you the answers you need to move into presenting the price and asking for a sale.

Pricing strategy has been around for many years and has been modified for all different types of industries. The idea is to strategically price your product in a way that gives you the best chance of selling your product or service. For example, 99 cents is more appealing than $1. When it comes to selling in-home construction services, it's usually best to use the good, better, and best strategy. Our objective is not to be the cheapest; our objective is to provide the best value while meeting all of our clients' needs. I can't tell you exactly how to price your services but it's a good idea to start with understanding your numbers as explained in a previous chapter. Your pricing should reflect the margin that you need to make to reach your company's goals.

Never try to compete on price. It's a recipe for failure. If you do a great job presenting your company and executing the process, then you shouldn't even be competing with anyone else. You're walking out with a deal today. It's always a good idea to have 2 to 3 different estimates with different prices and costs, but not different margins. When you present your estimate or price, you should present the best, most expensive option first and work down from there. Find the right price and value combination that works for your client without sacrificing profitability.

The most important factor in developing your pricing strategy is financing. I would encourage any company that sells any in-home construction services to find a financing company to partner with. There are many of them out there and it is not difficult to add financing for your company. Whether your clients use financing or not, you are drastically setting yourself apart. You are also increasing your odds of selling each deal. When you are asking about pricing and payments, you are giving the customer options. You are not giving them an easy "I can't afford it" or "It's more than I thought" excuse to not buy your service. If you can direct the conversation to payments, then you have essentially already closed the deal.

The close is simple. Remember the journey that you have been taking your client on through this entire process. When you have reached the point where you have presented your service and you have answered all their questions, before or after they asked them, and you have given them the pricing and payment options, all you have left to do is ask for the sale. You just have to ask. I know it seems elementary, but I have seen many people struggle with sales simply because they are too afraid to ask for the sale. Ask for the sale with confidence and reinforce that you are going to do everything that you said you were going to do. Ask them, "Which option would you prefer: A, B, or C?" Or ask them, "Which time slot would you prefer?" Remember: it's all about the process. Focus your energy on mastering the process and the sales will follow. Follow the process, ask for the sale, sign your paperwork, and move on to the next one.

Step 7: The Follow-Up

Just because you walked out of someone's home with an agreement to do work, whether it be by contract or verbal commitment, it doesn't necessarily mean that you got their business. Many states have laws that allow construction contracts to be broken within a certain time frame. Following up and quality communication are the most important aspects in all of our businesses, yet it is also where we, as contractors, fail the most. I could fill a room and ask if anyone has had a bad experience with a contractor and the majority would raise their hand. Nearly all would say that it was because of poor communication and lack of follow up. Nearly half of all salespeople never follow up and more that 25% never follow up more than twice.

It's a great idea to follow up with every customer regardless of whether you got a sale or not. If you did not get the sale, then you can send a thank you card or email them thanking them for their time and asking for any feedback to help you get better. I have always liked sending personal thank-you cards to every customer. This isn't a perfect science, and you're not going to get every deal. Following up is vitally important to increasing your overall closing ratio and efficiency levels. We like to use the 1,3,7,10 method when following up with clients who haven't committed. One is next-day follow up and can be a thank you card, call, or email. Three is three days after your meeting, when you want to just simply call and follow up to see if they had any more questions and to thank them again for their time. At 7 and 10 days you want to call again to find out if they have made a decision and you want to ask them when you should follow up again. Be sure to notate when they said to follow back up with them, put that in your calendar, then follow up as you said you would. You will be surprised at the results you get. People will compliment you on your diligence and professionalism and you will get more deals. Across all industries more than half of sales are made after the 5th follow up and hardly anyone in our industry follows up. The deal is not over if you don't get the sale right away. Separate yourself by being very good at following up.

If you did get the sale, then you will want to have a follow-up process in place that starts right away or right when the job gets entered into the system. They should receive a call or email thanking them for their business and informing them that their job has been submitted and is in process. The customer should also receive a call or message at each phase of their process: when their materials are ordered, when the crew is scheduled, when the inspection is done, etc. Customize this to your company's process. Many CRMs or software programs out there will allow you to automate this communication through email. Constant Contact and MailChimp are two examples of companies that specialize in email communications and automation. Again, this is the age of technology. Imagine if every customer receives automated emails keeping them informed about their project. Imagine what doors that could open for your production system and how many issues could be avoided. The cable companies do it…why can't we?

Automation is great but it still doesn't take away from human interaction. As a contractor, it is still very important to verbally communicate with your clients in addition to automation. You still want to be present when the project is under construction and maintain regular phone calls throughout the whole customer process. Following up is the key to growing your business. Not only does it help you close more deals, but great communication will increase efficiency and ultimately make your company more profitable.

Tracking and Accountability

One more important factor in executing a sales process and building a dynamic sales team is accountability. It is just as important to track everything and to hold one another accountable as it is to have a sales process in the first place. You can't have one without the other. The system is great, but how do you know how well it is performing? It's a great idea to track as many pieces of information as you can, especially when it comes to sales. If you can track it, you can measure it; if you can measure it, you can set goals to achieve it.

There are a number of different things that can be tracked and we are constantly looking for useful ways to collect data. We can use this data to measure performance. The way to do this is through KPIs or key performance indicators. The most obvious KPI would be closing ratio or, as we call it, success ratio. This is how we measure the rate at which a salesperson closes deals. It is calculated by dividing the number of presentations they give by the number of signed agreements they get. Many companies barely even track closing ratios. We want you to take it even further than that. We have built out a sales tracking platform that tracks numbers of leads, numbers of presentations, signed deals, booked revenue, closed revenue, efficiency, and average job size. We are able to track the salesperson's overall efficiency and focus our training on the different areas in which a salesperson might be struggling. We base these numbers on predetermined goals and track our sales teams progress towards their goals. This platform is a great way to keep your whole sales team on the same page and it's a great way create accountability and competition amongst your whole team. A competitive and accountable team is a productive team.

Here's an example of our sales team goal tracker dashboard. To get more information on our sales team tracker contact us at www.theroofingacademy.com or www.btacademy.com/sbgbook

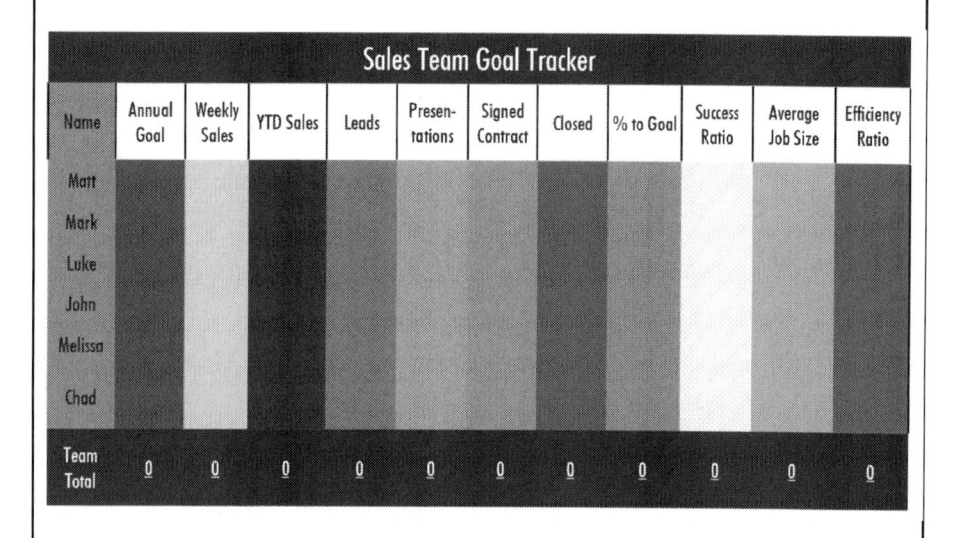

Name	Annual Goal	Weekly Sales	YTD Sales	Leads	Presentations	Signed Contract	Closed	% to Goal	Success Ratio	Average Job Size	Efficiency Ratio
Matt											
Mark											
Luke											
John											
Melissa											
Chad											
Team Total	0	0	0	0	0	0	0	0	0	0	0

Previously I've talked about how important it is to have great coaching on a sports team. What directly correlates with great coaching is practice. Practice, practice, practice. This doesn't mean just, "Here's a program, read over it." No. You want to role play. You want to have regular practice sessions with your team.. You need to be very involved or have a trainer or manager very involved, not only with teaching and training your sales program, but also with practicing your sales program themselves. If you're doing a PowerPoint presentation in someone's house and you're fumbling over your words and you're not able to be in sync with the slide that you're showing, you're not going to do a good job. So, how do you get better? You practice.

By practicing, I mean doing role playing. Practicing in front of a mirror. Practicing in front of a camera. Practicing with other teammates. Practicing with your managers. Practicing with your wife or with your kids. Do whatever you have to do to practice your craft so you can perform at a really high level.

I opened the chapter by describing the situation within our company before we had a sales process in place. After plenty of kickback and sales team turnover, our team eventually embraced the things that I've talked about throughout this chapter. They understand the difference between a salesman and an educator, consumer buying habits, and the psychology of the sale. They finally got on board with building out a sales process. By having a very detailed training program in place for our sales team, our performance as a company drastically changed for the better.

We not only were able to do more volume, but we were able to do more volume with fewer people. That's the objective. You want to be as efficient a company as you can possibly be and still achieve the goals you set. By having fewer salespeople who are very skilled and highly trained, you can protect that company reputation that you've worked so hard to establish.

CHAPTER 9
Marketing and Branding

Recently, I watched a show on MSNBC called *The Profit with Marcus Lemonis*. In his show he invests his own money into struggling businesses that need his financial and business help. In exchange for his investment, Lemonis gets an ownership percentage in the business and he takes charge of operations. It's a great television show, especially for entrepreneurs to learn what not to do in business and how to turn it around.

One business owner on that show had a product whose main target market was middle aged moms. The owner was using a $150,000 monster truck and swimsuit models to promote his product. His business was completely upside down and he was spending a ton of marketing money in the wrong places. He didn't understand that he was targeting the wrong demographic. You don't target a mom and her children with female swimsuit models. He completely missed the mark there. This is an example of bad branding and marketing.

Branding

Branding is super important to any business, especially if you want to build a business to last for generations. Consider some major companies that create brands that are familiar all over the world. Take anything from cereal brands such as Cheerios, to vehicles such as Chevy, to sports teams such as The Dallas Cowboys, or even motorcycle companies such as Harley Davidson. Some of these big brands have different brand promises that have been emphasized and marketed over time. Chevy suggests it makes the most dependable, longest lasting truck on the road. Charmin asserts it's the softest toilet paper. The Dallas Cowboys claim to be America's team. Harleys are for the rugged manly man. It blows me away that someone is willing to tattoo a big Harley Davidson symbol on their shoulder when it's just a motorcycle manufacturer. That is the power of branding. And branding is very powerful when done right. While this is certainly true for multi-billion-dollar companies and Fortune 500 companies, it's also true for our own individual construction trades companies.

When we first started, we had a very limited of budget for marketing and branding. We could barely afford a couple yard signs. But I knew the importance of it, and each year I continued to budget a little bit more, and a little bit more, until we got to the point where we built the really great brand that it is today—a household name in one of the biggest markets in the country. The place to begin when creating a brand for your company is with analyzing your company's mission and your company's values. Like all facets of your business, you should start there.

The purpose of branding is to differentiate yourself in the market no matter what widgets you're selling. Whether you're selling roofs, flooring, landscaping or you own a painting company, it's imperative that you differentiate your company from your competition. Regardless of your trade there is a lot of competition. There are many other companies out there that offer the same service or product as you do. The trick is to imprint your brand image in the market in a more effective way than the competition does.

Building a household name brand doesn't happen overnight, unless you have an unlimited budget and you don't care about profit. Branding is an ongoing process that you will probably be working on throughout the life of your business. There's a reason that big companies make adjustments to their branding on a regular basis. They need to stay fresh in the public eye. It starts with a logo, a slogan, and a brand promise or mission statement, but it evolves over time. You'll want to build a branding strategy that you can continually execute while growing your company.

Branding strategy is more than just titling your company and giving it a cool logo. It's about asking yourself questions that help you differentiate your company from everyone else. What is the message that you want to present to the public? Think about the details of the overall message you want your customers to hear. Does your logo and slogan represent you and your company's values? Can your logo be easily recognized? Is it the right color? Think about the color scheme that you want to have for your company. Is it something that you like? Are there any competitors that have the same colors? You can even take that thought process to a deeper level and do some psychological analysis of what the most attractive colors are to consumers. Some of the biggest companies spend a great deal of money on research and analysis to come up with their branding strategies. We don't have their budgets, nor do we need to spend a lot of money on it. We just need a simple brand image that represents our company in an effective way.

I have always liked the color red because it is eye-catching. Some people don't like to drive red cars because they feel like they're going to have a better chance of getting pulled over; others like to drive a red car because they want to be noticed. Before we decided on our company color we observed our local competition to see what colors they were using. We realized there weren't any major brands, in our market, that had red as their primary color. Therefore, we decided to go with red. It's a good idea to pay attention to what your competitors are doing to find ways to differentiate yourself.

You'll want to increase your brand recognition by using your same logo and colors across all marketing platforms. You'll want a logo that stands out for the right reasons; you don't want a logo that's too busy or too complicated. Some logos are downright unattractive or even offensive. A simple logo that you can build a brand around and one that people can easily recognize is what you want. Think of the Nike *swoosh*.

In order to execute your branding strategy you have to figure out the budget you have and the budget you need. Branding is different because there isn't a direct correlation between it and your return on investment. It's hard to see exactly what your ROI is for the logos you put on yard signs, trucks, etc. Budget a comfortable amount without overspending. Just know that the more effort you put toward branding, the more people will recognize your company. Even starting with a small budget, you can create a logo, make company shirts, and get magnets or window stickers for your trucks quite inexpensively. What you want to do is to make certain that you start with the right theme so that you'll be able to add on to that branding strategy as your budget grows. Changing logos or branding themes mid stream can be costly. When you add marketing items, you want to make sure to stick with the same theme, colors, and image. It takes multiple exposures to an image before someone recognizes it permanently.

Marketing

Branding and marketing go hand in hand. However, you want to look at them as two different parts of your business. Branding is an ongoing process of exposing your company to potential future clients. Marketing, however, is a direct action that tries to prompt or incentivize a customer to call you today to request your services. Marketing is active; branding is passive. Marketing is just as important to understand as is branding.

Over the years, I have learned a great deal about marketing and have spent a lot of money trying and find the best ways to market my companies. I enjoy marketing and being involved with it. There are many different ways to market your companies and they will vary from industry to industry. Here's my list of some of the most common ways to market construction companies along with strategies to make the greatest returns.

Canvassing

One of the age-old marketing strategies used by many home improvement and construction companies is called canvassing, otherwise known as door knocking. This is a tried and true marketing strategy and one of the least expensive ways to get your company started. It doesn't cost you anything to go knock on doors and tell people about your business and its effective because you're marketing directly to the consumer. You can pre-qualify your customer before you even knock the door. If you are selling windows, then you can look for houses that need windows. If you are selling roofs, then you want to go to a neighborhood that has lots of damaged roofs.

Canvassing can get expensive once you start hiring people to canvass for you. There are many successful companies that use canvassing as a primary marketing source, especially in the insurance restoration industry. If you want to use this method of marketing, it's a good idea to follow the same principles of building a sales team. Create a system and perfect that system. You will want to hire a canvassing manager that has the right characteristics to work in the field knocking on doors, getting doors slammed in their face, managing people, and dealing with lots of turnover. It is a difficult position to perform and fill, so pay the right amount and make sure you have the right person. If you hire canvassers, be aware that there will be great deal of turnover. Have a hiring process in place so you can always be hiring for this position. A properly structured canvassing team can be a very effective way to market certain companies. There are also many online tools and apps to use to track your canvassing team's production. Sales Rabbit and Spotio are two examples of canvassing apps currently in the market.

In some market situations, canvassing can be counterproductive and very difficult. If you're working in a market where you get a lot of weather events, such as hailstorms, then there will be many different companies canvassing the same areas you want to canvass. What can happen is multiple companies come into the same neighborhood and canvas the same houses. This creates a lot of chaos and confusion between homeowners. What homeowner likes getting their door knocked on over and over by different companies selling the same thing? Homeowners become overwhelmed with multiple canvassers at their door.

As a company that is focused on providing each customer with the best overall experience possible, we chose to stop canvassing this way. We prefer to canvass only neighbors of clients who we have already contracted. We call this six-packing. The salesperson will try and speak to both neighbors to the left and right of their customer and to the 3 neighbors across the street, therefore creating a six pack of houses. This is very effective when you can get your customer to take you to their neighbors houses. Do a great presentation and this will happen. It's much easier to sell a referral than a cold call.

Networking

Another inexpensive and very effective way to market your company is by joining a networking group. This is especially important when you are first starting out. There are many different groups to choose from. I recommend joining one that meets every week and has only one member per business category. There won't be multiple insurance agents, multiple roofers, multiple realtors, or more than one of any other category of business in the same group you're in. You want to find a group that has this sort of a structure so you're the only painter or the only roofing contractor, for example, in that group.

You'll want to find a group that has as members of other professions which complement yours. So, as a roofer, you want to be in a group that has an insurance agent, a real estate agent, and maybe a general contractor. You'll also want to be in a group which has other types of contractors who deal with homeowners daily. When a painter is bidding a job for a homeowner and notices the house needs a new roof, he can recommend your company or visa versa. These are very warm leads. Remember, the idea is to get as many referrals as possible. To make the most of networking, it is a good idea to understand that the more you put into it the more you will get out of it. You're there to help others build their businesses and they're there to help you build yours. You won't just start getting business right away. Be diligent with your attendance and build relationships with the other members.

Canvassing and networking are the two best, most effective, and inexpensive ways to start marketing your company, but the marketing doesn't end there.

Direct Mail

Regardless of your trade, you'll want to target certain size homes, certain aged homes, or a certain area of town that has more appealing projects. The best way to reach specific demographics with printed media is through direct mail. This type of marketing campaign can range from inexpensive to very expensive. If you decide to do direct mail, make sure the mailing is comparable to the rest of your company's branding and make sure you have good-quality content to deliver to those homeowners to differentiate yourself from the others in your business. There are many companies that can help you develop a direct mail campaign. Find the one that's right for you.

Website

This is the age of technology. Website and internet marketing is the future— and the future is now. The days where you could just run a Yellow Pages ad, or just go down to a local coffee shop, hang out with your buddies, and wait for them and others to recommend you for a job is over. We're in an age of technology, where the consumer is more educated than ever before. Anyone can learn anything about anything on the internet. It blows my mind to see how many construction companies have bad websites or no website at all.

Often, the consumer has already researched your company and has already researched the product they want before they call you. Therefore, as a business owner and contractor, you need to have a good-quality website. You can start a website virtually free by going online and creating your own. You can choose your own design, write your own content, and upload your photos very inexpensively. You want to make certain that if you are writing the content yourself that it is useful and understandable to a reader because it will have an effect on your website's ranking. If you have a bigger budget, or you keep growing and can increase your marketing budget, you should hire a professional to do it. This should preferably be someone that you know and trust, who has a good reputation with good references. They should also be very strong with search engine optimization (SEO).

Search Engine Optimization

SEO is a marketing strategy geared towards building your website around what consumers are searching for on the internet. Using search engine optimization helps you target your customers more effectively. If, for instance, you have a customer who is looking for a specific type of window and she types words or phrases relating to the window she's looking for into the Google search bar, the search engine analyzes those common words being searched to find a list of websites that is relevant to the customer's inquiry. The search can be made within your specific industry, or your specific segment of your industry, or limited to a certain geographical area. Websites are primarily ranked by how much traffic they get, how old they are, and by how easily they can be found through search. Google is the #1 most recognized search engine so I will focus my examples on Google marketing. Many of the same principles can be used across all the different search engine platforms.

There are a number of ways that you can market your website online. You can do it "organically" or you can pay to have your site put in front of people. Organic search results are those that naturally appear on Google in the main section of the search page. Organic exposure is based on content relevant to the keywords being searched. Organic exposure happens when you write content into your website, create blogs, or you build in links that contain the keywords that you are targeting. This type of content can get you exposure without having to pay Google. Organic exposure and growth comes with time and effort. You just have to continue to work at it; the more content you add to your site, the more visible on the internet your company will be.

Search engine optimization is based on a very complicated algorithm that Google is constantly updating and changing. Therefore, it's advisable that you hire a professional to help you with this process. This is probably the biggest and the most important investment you can make when starting your internet marketing strategy.

AdWords

Another way to generate traffic to your website is through AdWords marketing, which is paid advertising or paid exposure through Google. This can be an article, landing page, or a specific wording designed to target words relevant to what you're selling. You can target individual words that when searched, will automatically place your ad on the top or side of the page. The more popular your targeted adword is, the more money you're going to pay for each click. You're actually paying per click when doing Google AdWords marketing. A good marketing strategy for your website is to have a combination of both organic exposure and paid exposure. Have a good balance of these two things based on a budget that you're able to put forward. The goal is to get on the search engine's first page, then into the top 10, and eventually among the top three or the top five in as many search word terms as possible.

Online Reviews

Eighty-five percent of people check the internet before they make a purchase. It's a great idea to get as many reviews online as possible, hopefully good ones. There are a number of platforms or websites out there that do different reviews for products and services. There is the Better Business Bureau, Angie's List, Yelp, Google, Bing, and many others. As I mentioned earlier, we're in the age of technology; consumers are more educated than they ever have been, and with that education, comes power. It's very powerful when you have a customer write a positive comment online about your company.

The importance of getting your customer to review your company online cannot be over-emphasized. The more reviews you get, the more exposure you get, the more potential customers will read them, the better off your company's going to be and the faster it is going to grow. There are many different strategies to help you get more reviews for your company. You want to come up with a good strategy that works with your brand and your company to get those reviews.

Just like asking for the sale, it starts with simply asking your customer to write a review. Many of us just forget to ask or it's not a priority for our salespeople to ask. You can also have some sort of a promotional program where if a customer leaves you an honest review, they can earn a gift card or another incentive. You can create an ongoing referral program where if a customer gives you a referral, you give them points that can be redeemed at different levels. For example, each referral that buys your services will earn the referring person a point. Each point is worth a prize and the more points, the better the prize. You can have prizes such as a gift card, a TV, or even a trip. The key to getting reviews is that in order to redeem their points, the referring person must leave an honest review of your company. This approach has worked really well for us.

Social Media

Social media comes right behind having a good web page and having a good SEO strategy in level of importance. Having a great social media presence is very important. I don't know if you have noticed, but everywhere you look, everybody has a cell phone in his or her hand, and is constantly checking his or her phone, whether checking Facebook, Twitter, LinkedIn, or some other platform. People are staying connected with friends and family and with businesses. Social media has completely overtaken and changed the way we do marketing, not only in the construction industry, but in all consumer-based industries.

I recommend that you get on the social media bandwagon as soon as possible. There's still huge growth potential in this area. Social media is simply a platform, or media outlet, in which people communicate with one another. There are many platforms available, but you want to choose the one that best fits your target market. For instance, if you're trying to sell painting services, and your target market is first-time home buyers, you're targeting people between 25 and 35 who are buying new homes. You'll want to go onto a social media platform that tailors to that demographic. And right now, in that specific instance, it would most likely be Facebook. Facebook is the number one platform for social media, and Facebook advertising is going to be one of the most recognized, premier marketing outlets for every company in the near future. The reason for this is... data. Facebook has one of the biggest collections of data out there. Think about it, all they're doing is collecting data with every click on their site!

Every time somebody posts something, every time somebody likes something, every time someone shares something on Facebook, that data is collected. They're collecting that activity from every single individual to the point where you, as a business owner, now can target a specific person, a specific age bracket, or a specific neighborhood. When someone is talking on Facebook to their friends about wanting to get their new house painted, you can practically target that person directly. Facebook will make sure your ad pops up on their feed. You can do this on your own, too, by paying attention to what your friends and family are posting about. It's almost scary to think about how much data, and how much information, has been collected since Facebook has been in existence. I'm no social media expert or Facebook guru, but I do know that we get a lot of exposure and a lot of clients from Facebook.

Here are a couple more tips on how to build an effective social media campaign: The first is to have good-quality content. If you're always posting, "Buy my product, buy my product, buy my product," people are going to ignore it. On the other hand, if you're giving people good information about the product, good information about your services, or just a random tidbit that's funny, they will be more likely to read your posts. Gary Vaynerchuk wrote about this strategy in his book *Jab, Jab, Jab, Right Hook*. The premise of that book is to offer value to a potential customer through constant and quality content and information (jabs), then to hit them with a right hook or call to action. That right hook is asking that customer directly to buy your product or sign up for your service. For example, "I've already provided some value, now call me for the free inspection." So, you want to have a nice blend of good-quality content, good information, and then also a good-quality call to action to get them to want your services.

One word of caution regarding the use of social media for communication and for marketing: Social media is everywhere and can be seen by anybody. Keep in mind that every single thing you post online and every single piece of information you make public stays public. If you're having a bad day, or you got irritated because someone cut you off on the highway and you gave them the finger, or you wanted to complain and whine online to your friends, or your family, consider that the whole world can see it. It's a good idea to keep your personal thoughts and opinions offline. As a business owner, you are setting the example for your whole company. Be cognizant of every single thing you put online; you never know which potential customers or competitors might see it.

Marketing Plan

We discussed all the different types of marketing platforms and ways to market our companies. But how do we execute them? We execute them by having a plan. Just like we want to have a plan for our business and our life, we want to have a plan for each part of our business. We do this by creating a marketing plan. I want to illustrate a few ideas on what you need to do to create a plan. We all know that you have to do marketing and branding to grow your company. You also know that you need to have a website, engage on social media, and do other things that were covered in this chapter. But how do you plan for that? It starts by writing it down. Whether on a spreadsheet, a calendar, or a piece of notebook paper, start by illustrating your marketing ideas on paper. Plan out which ideas you will execute at which times during the year. Many trades businesses are cyclical because of weather changes. Plan your marketing strategies alongside your peaks in business. Have regular marketing meetings to help execute that plan on an ongoing basis. You'll want to have both short-term and long-term marketing strategies.

Within that plan, list all the different marketing channels that you're going to use. Start with checking all the marketing channels that you've used in the past and try to determine exactly what the return on investment for each of those marketing channels was. For instance, if you spent $500 on direct mail, and you got 10 deals from those postcards, you can calculate your return on that investment.

Not only can you can do this with direct mail, you can do this with the internet. When people click on your website, that data is tracked and you can figure out which ads and what efforts are getting customers to click on your website the most. It's very important that you have a tracking system in place. After listing what marketing avenues you plan to use, have a plan on how to track each lead source so you can calculate your ROI individually. You can start making adjustments every week, month, quarter, or annually as needed. You want to make certain that you are maximizing every dollar spent on marketing with the highest possible return on investment. It can be tricky tracking all your different marketing channels. It's a good idea to make sure that whoever answers your phone is asking where they heard about your company every time.

Now you want to create a budget to support your marketing plan, whether it's a couple hundred bucks a month, or a few thousand bucks a month. Start with a budget that fits your current cash flow and increase that budget as you grow your company. If you don't cashflow yet, then you'll want to keep this budget to a minimal. Use as many free methods as possible, i.e., networking and canvassing. I like to use a small percentage of my revenue to create my budget. You can get away with budgeting something between 1% and 10% of your total revenue depending on your business model, average job size, and gross profit margin. Most likely, you won't be able to divide the required amount by twelve months to figure out an equal amount to spend each month. Our work isn't spread out equally throughout the year. We don't do much exterior work in the winter, but in the summer, we double down and do as much as possible. After you plan your entire year to see when your busiest and your least busy times are, decide what marketing you want to do and how much you want to spend based on the expansion and contraction of your business volume. You'll want to budget more during or right before your busy season and scale the budget back during the slow season. For example, if you have a $250,000 company and you budget 5% you will need $12,500 to spend on marketing. If 75% of your volume comes in the summer then you will want to allocate 75% of your budget right before and during that time frame.

Once you have your budget set and your marketing outlets written down, you can create the plan. Use a calendar to track and execute the plan for each week, month, and year. A good marketing plan is very detailed. It includes exactly how often you're going to write a post, or how often you'll place an ad online. It will tell you when to launch a direct marketing campaign and when you'll order yard signs. You'll also want to be very specific regarding the how, and the timing of your online releases. The more detailed you can be in this marketing plan, the better off you're going be, and the better decisions you're going to able to make. For more information and examples of marketing plans go to www.btacademy.com/sbgbook or www.theroofingacademy.com

When thinking about marketing It's important to have a good upfront plan and strategy. It is also important that you have a good follow-up strategy as well. Once someone has inquired about your company, clicked on your website, or called your phone number, you'll want to track the information. You want to be able to stay in contact with that customer whether they buy from you or not. Collect their info including their email address. You can follow up with them from time to time to stay in their mind for the next time they might need your services. They might not buy from you now, but you may get them to purchase from you at a later date.

I believe that it's important for anyone in life and in any business to give back. Have some sort of budget to give back to your community and use your charitable contributions as part of the marketing plan. If you don't have a bunch of money to donate, give your time. You can donate your skills and abilities to nonprofits like Habitat for Humanity, for example. Giving back builds great morale and rapport with your staff. Consumers are going to want to support a company that gives back and cares about its community. Find something that's close to your heart or an organization that you can support while recommending that others show their support as well. Partner with them on your website and make sure that the public knows that it's important for your company to give back to the community. Participating in these or similar activities will support your marketing and your branding efforts.

When our company first started we had no money for a marketing budget. We barely had money for rent. We didn't know what we were going to do. I found a free website online where I created my own first logo design. I took it to a designer and I think I spent 60 or 70 bucks on it. We had one truck with a couple stickers on it, some business cards, and a very basic website. We continued to invest and make our website better. We documented the few projects that we did at the time and added those photos and videos to our website. Eventually, we were able to incorporate social media into our marketing plan. From there, we just added one piece at a time. We focused on getting better and better by creating more and more content and we built a great brand that is recognized throughout our state and now the country. One of the biggest things that really helped us was the rewards program that I explained earlier. Reviews are very important to your company's reputation and growth. Continue to focus on a branding and marketing strategy that represents your company's values, get your customers to post positive reviews, and you will build a great brand.

CHAPTER 10
Growing your Company

"My construction company is up and running, I have a full schedule of work, more estimates than I can count, and I'm busier than I've ever been. I don't have enough time or the money to hire more people, plus I can't find good help anyway, so I'll just do it all myself." I'm still handling the majority of the day to day operations and I'm the only one that can do it right, so I'll just work at night and, on the weekends to get caught up.

Does this sound familiar? This was me for the first 5 years after I started my construction company. I didn't have enough time to get all my payroll and billing done. I couldn't get my projects completed fast enough because I couldn't be on site all the time. Writing estimates at night and on weekends got old pretty quick, and orders were wrong because I couldn't double check them all. I spent more time at the Home Depot than I did at my own home. When I take a step back and look at this picture, all I had created was a job for myself and a pretty crappy one at that. I had to do something, I had to figure out how to get out of this "no man's land."

I call this place "no man's land" because it is a difficult place to be and can be a difficult place to get out of. You're not small enough to do it all on your own anymore, and you can't afford to hire enough people to justify the revenue that you are generating. You know that you need to increase sales and production capacity, but you just can't quite figure out how to make that happen without going broke.

There are many people who prefer to keep their companies fairly small, and they make a decent living. They make a life for themselves and are able to provide for their family. Many owners, however, want to scale their businesses. They want to hire people to do the work for them. They want to take off the hats and put them on someone else's head while maintaining profitability. After all, isn't the ultimate goal as an entrepreneur to work "on" your business and not "in" it?

I found myself in this so-called no man's land for years. I knew that it was not a sustainable option, but I didn't know how to get out. Through many long nights, weekends, and many mistakes, I have been able to reach a place of entrepreneurial freedom. My business runs itself and I work on growth and strategy while maintaining constant communication with all my department leaders. In order to get out of this place, you have to scale your company with a well executed strategy.

A couple of years ago, I came across a book called *Mastering the Rockefeller Habits* by Verne Harnish and it changed the way I thought about and ran my business. It was written several years ago, and has been revised recently with the new title *Scaling Up: How a Few Companies Make It...Why the Rest Don't*. These books are based on the business principles of John D. Rockefeller, founder of Standard Oil and deemed to be the greatest businessman in U.S. history. Both are great books written to help businesses get through scalability.

Three Phases of Growth

Every successful construction trades company goes through phases of growth along their journey. I've tried to simplify that process by illustrating three main phases. Phase one is the startup phase, the phase where you get to wear all the hats in your business. It's just you and maybe one or two other people. You wake up each day, and among other things, you have to figure out how to generate business, how to market your company, how to write the estimates, how to pay the bills, and how to coordinate the production side of your company.

It's important to not skimp on this phase because it has the biggest learning curve. You are learning about all aspects of your business. However, you don't need to be a master of every aspect. A lot of people struggle with this concept, but you'll have to accept it in order to grow. You don't have to know everything, but you do want to have experience within all facets of your business. When you're starting a business, you really need to know what it's like out there selling jobs, writing estimates, coordinating production, and dealing with the accounts payable and receivables. Make sure you have a good understanding of how the cash flow will work within your business. Cash is king. Phase one is the time from when you start the business to the time that you need to start hiring help to manage the workflow. For most contractors, this phase ends when the work gets to be more than 3 people can handle.

Phase two is the buildout phase. This is where you have to start thinking about the basic infrastructure of your company. This is where you start hiring the key people necessary to get your business to the growth phase. The buildout phase is equal in importance to the startup phase. In this phase, you're applying what you learned during the startup phase, when you wore all the hats, and hiring people to do those jobs you're not good at. You will probably hire a production manager, office manager, and/or a sales manager during this phase.

You may hire a sales manager to hire and manage a few salespeople if that's not your strength. In my case, I hired everything else first because my strength was in managing a sales team. You may hire a production manager and you may hire someone to help with the books, or an administrative person to run the office. The buildout phase is when you start building your foundation of great people who will help you grow your business. It's important that you find good-quality people. It's also important that you incorporate them in the inner workings of your business because these are the people who you're going to need to lean on to get you to the next phase: growth.

Phase three is growth, the phase where you start scaling your business into a company. You have built a solid foundation. You have some processes in place. You're producing at a consistent level, and you're learning and growing each day. During this phase, you build out your organizational structure, the management team that you hired in phase two is now starting the process of hiring people to work under them, and so on.

You may start adding more salespeople and production people. You are adding more and more skilled laborers. It's also important during this phase that you not only have your management team and organizational structure in place, but you also want to have deliverables and accountability measures in place. This will allow you to start holding your team accountable to work together to grow the company as a whole. Remember that people are motivated by recognition, not by discipline. Focus on their strengths, not their weaknesses.

This phase is also when you're going to really start refining your branding, marketing, and sales strategies. You should have consistent income and you should be able to allocate more resources towards branding and marketing. As your income increases, you'll want to invest more and more money towards the marketing, branding, and development of your business.

The processes will be in place to increase your volume without making major personnel changes. You should be refining the processes you have already created, not creating new ones. Most importantly, this is the phase where you switch from working in your business to working on your company.

Growth Plan

To properly scale your business, you have to plan. We've discussed planning in previous chapters, but in order to scale, you need to actually sit down and create a vision of where you see your business six months from now, nine months from now, and in one, two, three, and five years from now. Goals should be of many varieties and have both personal and monetary aspects. You should have achievable goals along with unachievable goals. Harnish even describes the BHAG, the Big Hairy Audacious Goal: an over-the-moon goal that could happen if everything went right and your company overachieved on a massive scale. Can your company be worth $100 million some day? Harnish says that it's okay to have a BHAG goal, because you want to always have a vision of what the future could be. That will help you stay on track and keep a vision of each step that it's going to take to get there. After all, if you shoot for the stars, you might just hit the moon.

You can't go from A to Z without all the rest of the letters. One key to start planning your business growth is to develop a one-page strategic plan for each year and each quarter. You want to illustrate your why, BHAG, values, goals, initiatives and the themes to help drive results. You have to answer these questions: Who are you going to need to help you reach your goals? What initiatives will it take to reach them? How much time and money is it going to take, and what are the critical numbers you need to focus on.

As you begin to scale your business, these questions have to repeatedly be asked and answered. To simplify this continual effort, Harnish created a one-page strategic plan that lists these questions and guides you to list out your answers in a meaningful way. One of my favorite sayings is, "You can only eat the elephant one bite at a time." That metaphor sums up what you're doing. You're trying to grow a big successful business and that project can seem similar in difficulty to consuming an elephant bite by bite. It doesn't happen overnight; it happens one step at a time. You can find Harnish's one-page plan at www.gazelles.com

Before starting your strategic plan, refer back to your organizational structure. What does your company look like right now? Does your company have only you or maybe one other employee? Now, contemplate what you want your company to look like in a year. Will the business include one helper, an office person, and maybe a marketing person? Or maybe a production person? Each business is different, so I can't give you an exact suggestion of what to do here, but I can suggest using our 5 pillars of a successful foundation as discussed in Chapter Five to get started.

After you envision your business a year from now, carry on this same exercise and plan what your business will look like two or three years from now. Try also to paint a picture of what your business is going to look like five years from now. What will your company look like when you have yourself, your partner, two or three managers, and a number of people working under those managers? What you want to do is give yourself a tangible chart, graph, or bubble chart of where your company is now, and where you plan for it to be in the near and distant future. The one-page strategic plan is going to keep you on track and on task with what you need to do.

Cash Flow Management

Many things are important to consider when scaling your business, but managing cash flow is the most vital. Cash flow is very important, and one of the first things I learned in business school was that cash is king. This is true more and more as my companies grow. Cash flow is especially tricky to manage in the construction industry. When you're doing construction projects that are spread out, you have to pay very close attention to when cash is coming in and when cash is going out. You can have a bunch of cash one minute and have absolutely none the next.

How do you plan for changes in cash flow? Start by analyzing what your current fixed expenses are on a daily, weekly, monthly, and annual basis. You should already have a business going, so you want to be able to determine what it takes every week, month, and year for your company to break even. At what point are your fixed expenses covered and you begin to make a profit? What does it take to cover your payroll, taxes, insurance, trucks, fuel, and all those other fixed expenses that are involved in running a construction company? Take all your monthly fixed expenses, divide that by the number of weeks, and then you'll get an idea of exactly what it's going to cost to operate your company each week. Example: If your total fixed expenses are $24,000 per month, you know that it costs you roughly $6,000 per week to operate your company.

Next, try and figure out how many projects are being produced each month and what all the variable costs are for those projects. These costs primarily consist of materials and labor. If your produced revenue is $100k each month and your variable costs are $60k, you can determine that your weekly outgoing cash to produce your jobs is $15k.

To determine how much cash you will need on a weekly basis, you can add the average fixed expenses ($6k) to the average variable costs ($15K) to determine your weekly cash demand ($21k). In this example, it takes a minimum of $21k per week to operate this company. This same formula can be used to determine your monthly, quarterly, and annual cash flow demands.

Make sure to do whatever it takes to have that money available every week. It will be tricky at times. When you're growing, it's hard to meet all your business financial obligations at the same time. You'll also have to pay for materials to maintain a copacetic relationship with your suppliers. You might also have varying subcontractor bills from week to week. It's hard to account for all the variable costs but if your have a good grasp of what your fixed costs are you can find ways to pay for growth.

If you see that the money you're bringing in doesn't cover your expenses, you can start making decisions like cutting back on production or borrowing money from the bank. You can put a greater emphasis on closing certain projects that may be lingering or uncollected? Maybe you just haven't put in enough effort to collect your outstanding A/R. Monitoring your cash flow on a regular basis will help you make better decisions and help you project your future cash needs.

We all go through it as entrepreneurs and as contractors. The cash demands that we sometimes face are really tough. As a business owner, there have been many a times I didn't even get paid. There also have been times that I've worried that we didn't collect enough money to pay the vendors or even pay the staff. I've worried, too, whether I would have enough money to pay for marketing. If I can't pay for marketing, how could I grow my company? These are some of the concerns that all entrepreneurs and business owners have, but the key to overcoming these concerns is in knowing where you are and envisioning where you want to go. When cash is heavy, invest it in growth. When cash is lean, focus on getting more cash.

When scaling your business, it's also a great idea to build solid banking relationships. When you first start out, you're not going to be able to just walk into a bank and get a loan. Construction, especially, is a high-risk business, and banks aren't just going to hand out money to small construction trades companies. If you want to scale your business, you're eventually going to have to figure out how to have enough cash reserved, how to borrow enough cash to hire people, and how to market and develop your company.

It is a good idea to start a banking relationship right away and build on that relationship. The bank may only lend you a couple bucks early on, but you can build from there. Make sure to always pay your loans on time. You will eventually want to get a line of credit, and then make sure that you're using that line of credit appropriately, always paying it down.

Say it's only a thousand bucks to start off; you pay that down a couple times, then you get to $5000. Pay that down a couple times, then you go to $10,000. Pay that down and you can eventually build a relationship to where, as your company grows, your credit lines grow. Having a good banking relationship will give you that cushion that you'll need to scale your company into a 5, 10, or 15-million-dollar company.

Another piece of advice I learned the hard way is don't take too much money out of your company. In fact, you won't want to take any money out of your company until you know it is in a comfortable financial state. This is where a lot of contractors and business owners fail. They see all this money going into their account, and they don't think about what it's going to cost to operate that company or to grow it. They see $50,000 in their account, and with little or no thought, withdraw $5,000 for a house payment, or a boat payment, or whatever they think they might need. Suddenly, bills come due. The owners have already spent that money, and now they can't pay their bills. This is one of the biggest reasons why companies fail; they don't plan and understand what kind of cash flow is needed to grow and sustain their business. When starting a business, be mentally prepared to be the first in and last to leave—and last to get paid.

Teamwork and Leadership

If you want to build a big, successful, high-growth business, you can't do it on your own. You know the old adage, "It takes a village?" It is absolutely true; it takes people, and it takes teamwork. Many companies get to this point of scalability where they want to scale up but they don't have the right people in place. Unfortunately, many others go backwards and they end up failing because they don't build their team the right way. You want to think of your employees as a team. And as you build out that team, you want to make sure that you have enough skillsets to handle all the different aspects of the business. It's of the utmost importance to have them working as a team. Companies will not grow and will not be successful if they don't act as one cohesive unit.

Another aspect of this, which I talked about earlier, is company culture. I'm a firm believer that a company's culture is created and ingrained by their leadership. Starting from day one, you want to start the process of hiring people who fit seamlessly into the culture that you've created. That culture should be a direct reflection of your company's mission statement and principles. You want to make sure to always stay true to your mission as a company. If you're spinning your wheels by hiring and training and having turnover due to a mismatch with corporate culture, you're not going to be able to grow and scale your business.

Remember to think of yourself as a leader and not as a manager. People don't want to be managed; they don't want to be told what to do, and they don't want someone looking over their shoulder every day. People want to be challenged, and more importantly, they want to be acknowledged when they do things right.

Revert back to my previous discussion on servant leadership. Servant leadership is a business leadership philosophy that shares power and puts the needs of others, your employees, first to help them develop and reach their highest potential. This type of leadership philosophy has been a key component to the success of our business and may be a key to the success of your business as well. The way to approach every day is as if you work for your team. You will start thinking about things differently; you're mindset will change and you'll get to a place where everyone on your team is working together as one unit. You have to have the right people in place before you can start making the leap from "in" to "on". We're all on this journey together, there's no point in climbing to the top of the business mountain by yourself. It gets lonely up there, you might as well bring as many people as you can. One of my favorite sayings is, "Embrace the journey, because the journey is the destination."

One of the most important things I've learned about scaling a business, and the reason I got my company over this "no man's land" hump is that scaling your business starts with people; it takes a well executed strategy and the right amount of cash.

CHAPTER 11
Transitioning from *In* to *On*

*I*t's monday morning; I'm ready to take on the week. I have a plan to get some much-needed things done that I have been putting off. I'm going to work on some new marketing ideas and I'm going to look over last quarter's numbers to figure out where I can save some money. I also want to follow up on a few estimates and invoices I sent a few weeks ago. The phone rings. It's my subcontractor and he needs some materials for the job. There's no one else available so I'll have to go get them. On my way there, I get a call from my office and I need to stop there to deal with some urgent issues. Before I know it, the day is over and I haven't had a chance to sit down and work on my list. No worries, I still have the rest of the week. Tuesday morning, I get a call to go look at a new job. Ok, I'll run out there as soon as I'm done checking on the job I have in progress. By the time I'm done checking a few jobs and measuring the new one, I get back to my office and it's already after noon. I'll try to get the estimate written up before the end of the day. I still have a couple more days to get to my list. Wednesday comes. That estimate still needs to be finished because I couldn't get it done yesterday. The phone rings..."

Does this story sound familiar? As contractors, we wake up and our day starts with the phone ringing and someone on the other end needing something. Our projects need our attention. We had a plan, a list of things to accomplish, but the next thing we know, we have spent our entire week playing defense, fielding calls, and putting out everyone else's fires while ignoring the things we wanted to get done. It's easy to get tangled in this habit of playing defense while wearing all the hats in our business. Things just keep piling up and the burden gets heavier and heavier. This is the typical day or week for many contractors. In the construction world, when you're managing a lot of different things at once, projects, business functions, subcontractors, vendors, and employees, it's very easy to get caught up in the chaos of the day to day and never actually have time to work *on* your business.

To remove yourself from the day to day operations and to work *on* your business and not *in it,* you have to start by setting aside specific uninterruptible time that is focused solely on your business strategy. You have to have to set achievable goals with measurable outcomes and you'll need a team of people that work together with proper accountability measures in place. It doesn't happen overnight, but with a step by step, day by day approach, you can build your championship winning company one piece at a time.

Time Management

The key to getting away from this defensive way of working and out of the rat race is through effective priority and time management. Time management is at the top of the list for the success of any entrepreneur. I've done a lot of research on business and I've read a lot of books by many different successful entrepreneurs. There's one thing they all have in common: They all attribute their success to the priority they place on their time. They are able to run multiple businesses, employ hundreds of people and manage a host of other responsibilities because they've mastered the art of time management. Every minute of every day counts.

In order to get better with your time management you have to work at it. At the beginning of each week, wake up and create a list of the top ten things that you want to accomplish that week. Next, ask yourself which of those ten things can you delegate? Which of those ten things can you push off to a later time? Which of those ten things need to be done immediately? Based on your answers, rearrange that list from the highest priority to the lowest. This new list will give you a good basis to begin assigning value to your time. Delegate those items that you can, and then start the process of blocking off time to tackle the remainder of your list one item at a time. This isn't an exact science and you won't be able to do this every day, but it's a good idea to start this process at least once a week and increase it from there.

Block scheduling is also an important part of effective time management. The purpose of block scheduling is to create time blocks within your weekly schedule that are dedicated to a specific purpose or specific tasks that you wish to accomplish. This is a strategy that you want to adopt as an owner and you'll want to implement with your team. Block scheduling is one of the procedures or processes you'll want everyone in your company to institute. You can call this a cadence or personal schedule—a daily and weekly schedule of tasks that you can add to or subtract from as you complete them.

When building a block schedule, it's important to plan for the randomness. As contractors, we're busy and must deal with different things that come up. We're putting out fires all the time. If you're not careful, these things can take over your schedule easily. You're most likely not going to be able to have a fully functioning block schedule from the get go. You can start by allocating just a few hours a week to the projects that you want to work on for your business. You want to put that time block in your schedule and leave it in your schedule.

Make yourself unavailable during those times. Start with a couple hours a week and increase from there. Make sure you use those time blocks effectively, and you'll eventually figure out how to free up more and more time. You'll be able to allocate more and more hours each week of uninterrupted time to the important things that you want to accomplish for your business.

Here's an example of my personal block schedule. It was a bit challenging to get used to at first, but I've learned to be completely dependent on it. If it's not on my schedule, it doesn't get done. I have grown into this schedule over time and it requires constant adjustments. This schedule is really a guideline for me to follow each week as I build and grow my companies. It allows me the ability to stay in tune with what's happening in all facets of company while also affording me time to work on my other business projects.

Block Schedule

	Sunday	Monday	Tuesday	Wednesday	Thursday	Friday	Saturday
6:00 AM	Sleep	Workout	Personal	Workout	Personal	Workout	sleep
7:00 AM		Meeting Prep	Service Meeting	Drop Off Kid	Drop Off Kid	Drop Off Kid	
8:00 AM		GSR Meetings	Flex				
			Meeting Prep				
9:00 AM			Staff Meeting	SBG Book	The Roofing Academy (TRA)		
10:00 AM	Church	Flex	Leadership Team Meeting			Personal / Golf	
		Meeting Prep					
11:00 AM		Sales Meeting	Flex	Flex	Flex		
12:00 PM		Lunch	Lunch	Lunch	Lunch	Lunch	Family
1:00 PM		Flex	Meeting Prep				
2:00 PM	Football	Review Weekly Reports	Coaching Session	Film TRA Videos	Field / Flex	Office / Flex	
3:00 PM		Update MBP	Flex				
4:00 PM		Flex					
5:00 PM		Pick-up kid	Pick-up kid	Pick-up kid	Pick-up kid	Pick-up kid	
6:00 PM	Family	Family	Family	Family	Family	Family	

Notice the flex time, the specific meeting time, and the personal time. I try and maintain a balanced schedule by taking into consideration these three components. The specific meeting times are time that I am working on my business while staying up to speed with everything that is going on in my company. The flex blocks are very important as they can be filled with a variety of things. I try and always have some sort of business project that I can work on when my flex time doesn't get filled with day to day issues or field work. The most important block of time that most people fail to commit to is their personal time. Personal time is *your* time. It's time for you to plan, think or shut down for a specific period. Taking this time for yourself will help you keep your sanity while encouraging you to work smarter, not harder.

Before you know it, you'll have a detailed schedule where you're able to effectively manage your time between working on your business, dealing with issues within your business, but most importantly, you're able to allocate time for yourself and for your family. The goal is to figure out what the best use of your time is and to focus as much of it as possible on the things that directly correspond with the growth of your company. Delegate the regular day-to-day tasks as much as possible.

Goal Setting

It doesn't matter whether you have two people on your team or twenty, you want to make sure to implement a regular regimen of team meetings. I know everyone hates meetings; meetings can be very unproductive and boring if they are not executed well. As long as you have a structured meeting with an agenda, they can be quite productive and essential to any company's growth. In order get to a place where you are fully working on your business you must have a structured management team in place and regular meetings with that team. You'll want to start at the top management level, such as department heads, and have weekly meetings with them. Those managers should then have a weekly meeting with their team members. Your whole team should have a meeting with their corresponding manager every week or at least every other week.

We always like to make goal setting and review the main focal point of all meetings. We call our meetings GSR meetings or goal setting and review meetings. The GSR is a meeting in which you or your management meet with an individual or group with an agenda for reviewing the previous period's goals and set new goals for the next period. To implement GSR's within your meetings, explain what the GSR is, explain what your company's goals are, then let each person set a goal that corresponds with the company's goals. You'll also want to have GSR meetings individually with your staff because you will have the opportunity to connect on a deeper level. Make sure to write down each person's goals. We prefer using a spreadsheet that has each meeting date and each person's previous goal and current goal illustrated in combination with a written agenda. At every meeting we all review our previous week's goals and set new ones. We like to highlight the goal in green when the goal was hit, highlight in orange if the goal was not quite hit, and in red if it wasn't hit at all. This works well because no one wants to get a red.

A goal shouldn't be, for example, "I want to get better at my job" You want to set goals based on what's called KPIs, or key performance indicators. Using key performance indicators is an objective way to evaluate the success your company has in reaching its goals. These are directly correlated to your company's outcome. These KPIs are usually number related; in other words, the goal has to be able to be measured by a number. They should be related to your overall business performance and they should be correlated with the company's goals . They can be specific numbers such as: gross revenue, gross profit, or net profit related. They can also be time related and geared towards things like increasing the time it takes from selling a job to closing the job or the time it takes to complete a project. KPIs can also be related to things such as specific processes within each department. The objective is to have specific trackable indicators with measurable outcomes; critical numbers that you can use as a basis to set goals.

It's very important to start at the top. Set your company goal first and make sure your whole staff understands what that goal is. Establish key deliverables and KPI's for the company to help your team understand what they need to do within their capacity to help the entire company reach its goals. An example of this might be that for the first quarter of the next year, the company goal is to reach $1,000,000 in revenue with a 40% gross profit margin and you want all the jobs closed within 60 days. You will want everyone in the company to know and understand this goal. Each person will want to set their goals to feed into the overall company goals. If the billing person is setting a goal, it might have something to do with getting a certain number of invoices out within a certain time frame. If a sales manager is setting a goal, it might be related to increasing the profit margin on each job. The objective here is to have the whole company moving in the same direction with similar goals in mind.

Strategic Management and Accountability

To ensure that meetings are productive and goals are being achieved, there has to be accountability measures in place. You can force people to attend meetings, you can implement block scheduling, and you can give people KPI's, but if you don't have accountability measures in place, it's all going to fall apart. The glue that holds this strategic management together is accountability, and it starts with you as the owner. You should have specific deliverables each week and each month that you have to get done. Figure out what the critical numbers are that your business must reach in order to reach your goals. These critical numbers are most likely related to sales and profitability. For me it starts with tracking every job that closes each week. I review all the closed jobs each week and I update them into my master business plan file. I also require that each department head provide me with a weekly report based on specific numbers I want tracked each week: number of jobs booked, produced and sold; total revenue, and gross profit % to be more specific. Your team should have certain requirements based on their KPI's that are required to get done within specific time periods.

Once you have accountability measures in place, you'll want to have coaching sessions with your team. Use these meetings as 1-on-1 development sessions with your key team members. Train your managers to have coaching meetings with their direct reports as well. Coaching is different from managing in that it is focused more on personal and professional development rather than day to day tasks. During your coaching session make sure to identify what that person's strengths are and what their areas for improvement are. Reinforce what they are doing well and always leave room for improvement. You build a great company by developing the people within your team. You also want to leave every meeting with next steps or specific things for your employee to work on. Even if it's uncomfortable for you, it's a good idea to give them more and more responsibility, and let them make mistakes. Also, Let them make decisions on their own. They will learn faster and take ownership of their position and responsibilities. In order to remove yourself from the day to day, you have to empower your team to make decisions without you.

The last piece of a strategically managed company is employee reviews. All corporate companies have regularly scheduled reviews with their employees. Employee reviews should be pre-planned and have a tangible report to go along with the pre-scheduled meeting. This report should account for any deliverables that the employee is responsible for and illustrate their performance grade within each one. There should also be a "keep doing what you're doing" section and a "room for improvement section." The employee should always leave a review with new goals set and positive encouragement. We like to have a 1-month, 3-month, and 1-year review with each new employee. We also have an annual review every subsequent year thereafter. The employee review is an opportunity to reward your employee with a bonus or raise. Make sure the employee knows that they have reviews and when they will have them. This will help keep them focused and working hard because they know they are going to be graded and possibly rewarded for their efforts.

It's important to treat GSRs, coaching meetings, and employee reviews separately. They each serve their own purpose and should support one another, but not be treated the same. The GSR should measure and track ongoing goals and performance. The coaching meeting should be geared toward personal and skills development. The review should be treated as a way to evaluate and grade each employee's performance as a whole.

Business Coaching

One of the biggest challenges owners have to overcome is the expectation by their employees that, since they're the boss, they have to know everything. You're expected to have all the answers, but often, you don't. I don't. I'm still learning new things every day. I don't have all the answers. Who holds me accountable? For this reason I recommend that you humble yourself and recognize that you don't know everything and that you need other peoples' guidance to learn more. It's hard to be objective about yourself, but knowledge is power and you can't get more knowledge without learning from others. It's a good idea to find a business coach or a coaching program where you can be held accountable while continuing to master your craft as an entrepreneur.

It wasn't until I bit the bullet and partnered with a great business coaching platform that I was finally able to make the full jump from working *in* my business to working *on* my business. I was already on my way with a high volume company and some key people in place, but I still couldn't quite let go and let the business soar. I knew that I needed to get some sort of strategic management structure in place, we needed to have a system and process in place for everything, and we needed the right people in the right positions in order to fully step away from the day to day operations.

The Breakthrough Academy provided me with all the tools and coaching that I needed to get to a place of true entrepreneurial freedom. A place where my company runs itself while still knowing how each department is performing each week without having to be there everyday. It's a place where I can focus on growing my company while exploring other entrepreneurial endeavors.

Final Thoughts

Today, I'm sitting here writing this book while my companies hum right along. My journey from working in my business to working on my business has brought me to a place where I get to spend a large amount of my time sharing that journey with others. I wrote this book to use my story as an inspiration to the next generation of construction trades entrepreneurs. I want to encourage you to know that anything is possible regardless of the hands you are dealt in life. I want to help you find success without making all the same mistakes I did. This book is designed to be a blueprint to help guide your business from startup to scalability. I'm still on my journey and I'm still learning new things every day. My company's success has come from embracing the journey, learning from my mistakes, and implementing all the things discussed within the chapters of this book. My hope is that you will able to take away some things from this book that will help guide you as you embark on your entrepreneurial journey. Work hard, put others first, lead by example, learn and grow everyday, and, you, too, will find success.

Made in the USA
San Bernardino, CA
23 October 2018